GW00671942

Red Devil
Able Company
Double Dynamite

An Old Man's Memories
of World War Two

By Lawrence R. Nickell ASN 35768439

BEST WISHES TO
DICK AND MOLLY HIKES

Lawrence Nickell

Eggman Publishing, Inc.

© 1996 Eggman Publishing, Inc. All right reserved.

Written permission must be received from the publisher before using or reproducing any portion of this book, other than for the purpose of critical reviews or articles.

For interviews and other information call:
1-800-396-4626

ISBN: 1-886371-14-8

Eggman Publishing, Inc.
3012 Hedrick Street
Nashville, TN 37203
(615) 386-0133

Red Devil

Dedicated to the men of the Fifth Infantry Division,
who died that we might be free.

Solemn the drums thrill: Death august and royal
Sings sorrow up into immortal spheres.
There is music in the midst of desolation
And glory that shines upon our tears.

They went with songs to the battle, they were young,
Straight of limb, true of eye, steady and aglow.
They were staunch to the end against odds uncounted,
They fell with their faces to the foe.

They shall not grow old, as we that are left grow old;
Age shall not weary them, nor the years condemn.
At the going down of the sun and in the morning
We will remember them.

   For the Fallen
   Lawrence Binyon

Table Of Contents

The Ardennes Campaign

Back to the Rhineland Campaign

Central European Campaign

Maps

Foreword

This is a strictly personal account of my experience as a young man in the era of the Second World War. It is not a unit history. It certainly has no redeeming social value and the historical events have been recorded, endlessly and repetitively, by others in a much more literate manner. Probably the best thing that can be said about it is that you may rest assured that it is the last time I will attempt such a project. Also, the paper should be recyclable.

I think these events may be characteristic of the experience many young men had in those years. Kurt Vonnegut, who was an infantryman himself in that war, subtitled his book *Slaughterhouse Five* as *A Children's Crusade* and in many ways the war was a children's crusade. I was a teenager until the time my personal war ended, in a manner of speaking, and many of the men in my company were also teenagers. War is a young man's game, if you can call it a game, as the physical stress in a rifle company was too much for many older men, though some in their thirties held up remarkably well and I freely acknowledge that. I wrote this primarily to leave a bit of a record about what that war was like for this now old man for my grandchildren to read some day, should they wonder about it. I suppose autobiographical data is the ultimate ego trip. So be it. I have taken the opportunity during a period of convalescence from surgery to compile this tale. It is not all about combat. Some of it is about civilian life as a high school and college student, the good years in most people's lives, as they were in mine.

A fair amount of this is written in the years 1992-93 from memory but I wrote a rather detailed account of these events in 1945 after I came home and have largely relied on it, as well as histories of the Second Infantry Regiment and of the Fifth Infantry Division which are often quite detailed. I make no claim that dates, etc. are always correct but they are as accurate as I can recall them. General S. L. A. Marshall made the comment in his autobiography that the memory of combat events is often erroneous, even in the first few hours after the event. I find my current memory of the events described below is occasionally at variance with the events as I wrote them down in 1945. I have relied more on the old notes than my current memory. The events that took place in France I recorded in 1945 in considerable detail. My notes of events after we left France were somewhat sketchy but helpful in recalling some of the main events in the Ardennes and Germany. Some events I suspect I will never forget.

Gertrude Nickell, my sister in law, a year or so before she died gave me some letters from me that she had saved. I was a bit more candid about my fears in my letters to her and my brothers than to my parents, my father being in poor health at the time. Parts are excerpted and are interesting, to me at least, as they reflect my change in attitude about the war. They are printed in italicized script to avoid confusion with the rest of this tale.

A word in regard to the title. Able Company, as one might suspect, was the phonetic name for A Company. Double was the code name for the Second Infantry Regiment and Dynamite the code name for the Fifth Infantry Division. Don't think the names are descriptive of me though this is a personal account. I wasn't even a firecracker, certainly not dynamite.

The "fuzzy" pictures and maps were largely copied by computer from the Second Infantry Regimental History and were much better in the original publication. As this is not an art exhibit I have left them as is.

The cartoons are by Bill Mauldin from his book *Up Front*. The first one expresses an idea I suppose we all had but few self supporting persons have had time to carry it out.

"You'll get over it, Joe. Once I was gonna write a book exposin' the army after th' war myself."

Red Devil

Innocence

On the idle hill of summer,
Sleepy with the flow of streams,
Far I hear the steady drummer
Drumming like a noise in dreams.

Far and near and low and louder
On the roads of earth go by,
Dear to friends and food to powder,
Soldiers marching, all to die.
Housman-A Shropshire Lad

December 7th, 1941.

An ordinary mild late fall sunny Sunday afternoon became an extraordinary one, a red letter day. On it occurred the greatest jolt to complacency in American history.

On that fateful day we had crossed the street from my home to the little red brick Christian Church, eaten the usual Sunday lunch of fried chicken, mashed potatoes, rolls and peas and gone to the movie theatre. I don't remember the name of the movie that was playing that Sunday afternoon at the Rex Theatre in my home town of West Liberty, population one thousand, in the east Kentucky foothills. It makes little difference; it probably was one of the old Frank Capra movies that had a message about the value of honesty and character, so different from those of today with their themes of violence, obscenity and hopelessness. It is a little odd that I don't remember the movie since I can recall most of the events of the day quite well. The innocence of the American public and my own innocence were about to be destroyed for all time.

I was sixteen years old, a junior in the Morgan County High School, a fair student but more interested in the upcoming basketball season than in international affairs. Like most Americans at that time, I thought that the Japanese would never dream of starting a war with us and had argued with classmates about the superiority of American arms in the event of a war with the Japanese. I assumed that we could handle them with ease, a not uncommon but very erroneous assumption. In fact, I was absolutely certain (that means wrong at the top of your voice) that America could defeat the Japanese in a few days. Overconfident? Boy, oh boy! But I had lots of company. A few days? Yamamoto himself thought the Japanese would lose the war in a year and a half as did the English naval war correspondent Hector Bywater who may well have, in his publications, inadvertently given Yamamoto the key to the successful attack on Pearl Harbor. In the end it took almost four years to defeat the Japanese.

Were we interested in the war in Europe? Of course! It was the focus of America's attention. I still distinctly recall selling "extra" newspapers to the traveling salesmen in the old white frame Cole Hotel dining room the day the Germans broke out of the Ardennes in 1940 and clearly were soundly defeating the Allies. I had an evening newspaper route and, as I recall, I sold more extra newspapers than I had available and had to go back around my route and collect papers that some of my earlier customers, relatives of mine, had read so that I could deliver them to the customers on the end of my route. The extra bike riding, my first experience at recycling, double pun intended, and newspaper scrounging probably earned me an extra twenty- five or thirty cents. Capitalism pays! As a comment on prices at the time, the daily Lexington Leader sold individually for five cents a copy and a meal at the hotel with choice of country ham, steak, fried chicken or all three, with fresh rolls, cornbread, vegetables and dessert, all you could eat family style, was seventy- five cents.

The blitzkrieg campaigns of the German armies in Poland, Norway, the Low Countries and France would have impressed anyone but to us Europe seemed a very long way away. The Congress had voted to extend the draft by only one vote only two months before Pearl Harbor. I didn't know, and I doubt that one American in a thousand knew, that my future military unit, the Fifth Infantry Division, had sailed for Iceland, officially in the European Theatre of Operations, in September and October of 1941. American warships were escorting convoys in the North Atlantic and we were unofficial belligerents but few paid much attention to the Japanese aggression in the Pacific. After all, Christmas was coming up and embargoes and diplomatic shenanigans were not matters of great interest, especially to sixteen year olds.

Some of the local interest in the European War was undoubtedly related to the fact that the First World War was still a vivid memory, ending only twenty-two years earlier. The population in Morgan County was largely of old Scots-Irish or Anglo-Saxon stock, predominately rural, and many local men had keen memories of their participation in that war. One of my brothers, a brother- in-law and an uncle had served and one of my cousins, David Blair, for whom I was tentatively named, was killed. Many local men were decorated veterans and were highly regarded as a result. Nearby Breathitt County (so called "Bloody Breathitt" because of a reputation for feuding) had fulfilled its draft quotas in the First World War entirely by volunteers. Most local men prided themselves on their ability as marksmen. There were already a fair number of volunteers for military service. The country was just beginning to come out of the depression and a "hitch" in the service was a not too unpleasant alternative to the hard physical labor of subsistence farming that many local young men had to look forward to, even though a private's pay at the time was only fifty dollars a month, just increased from twenty- one dollars. The average attitude was not one of pacifism but , somewhat typical of the area, one of not "sticking our nose in other folks' business".

My nephew, Merle Nickell, and I came out of the theatre that well remembered sunny December afternoon and were surprised, along with everyone else in America, with the news of the attack on Pearl Harbor. There was scepticism at first as everyone remembered the infamous Orson Welles radio broadcast of the bogus invasion of the Martians from outer space only a few months earlier. The news initially was quite fragmentary, the networks for the most part continued their regular broadcasts, soap ads and all, but it soon became apparent that the attack was the real thing.

The memory of the president's broadcast referring to the "day of infamy" is still quite vivid. We older students sat in the back of the school gymnasium while the grammar school and junior high students sat toward the front. The sunlight, streaming in from the south, lit up the dust motes and it seemed quite unreal as we sat there on that beautiful late fall day in the rural Kentucky foothills and listened to the radio on the red and gold curtained stage call for a war that would involve so many of us. I'm sure there must have been someone in that age group who might later have been 4F (ineligible for service for physical or mental reasons) but I can't recall any. It all seemed unreal and far away but our world was tilting slowly and inevitably toward Mars. The drum beat was muffled but growing louder.

Four days after Pearl Harbor Hitler made his greatest mistake of the war when he declared war on the United States. We probably would have concentrated all our war effort on Japan rather than on Germany, had he not done so, and he may have won the war.

The rest of my junior and senior years passed uneventfully. The war news was followed with great interest. It was obvious that my class and some subsequent classes would have a personal military involvement but we made the most of our period of grace. The high school six man football team (we barely had twelve men for a scrimmage), basketball, baseball, fishing and hunting seasons kept us preoccupied. The high school team was nicknamed the "Red Devils" which, oddly enough, was also the a nickname for the military unit in which I later served. Life for us went on as before with the exception that "joy riding" in the family car was a thing of the past due to gas rationing. It didn't make a lot of difference as very few high school students had a car then anyway. The Depression was still with us, though alleviated to a marked degree by the buildup of the arms industry, and a two car family was a rarity.

Some of us helped work in "Victory Gardens" as an aid in the war effort. My father, brother, two nephews and I tended two or three acres of garden and Mom canned hundreds of cans of beans, tomatoes etc. We gave away far more than we kept. Meat, butter, sugar and cigarettes were rationed but there was no food shortage locally! Hard work in the garden in the morning and the afternoon in the old swimming hole, fishing or on the baseball diamond was an ideal life for a boy.

I suppose we were, in a way, incredibly lucky in that most families in that small community were interrelated, intact with little divorce and we were rather closely scrutinized so that there was not a great deal of juvenile delinquincy.The idiocy of television had not yet destroyed the art of conversation in the home or with the neighbors. We had a sense of clan or family and of belonging which seems to have disappeared. We had a basic ingrained feeling that we were part of a community that cared for us as we cared for them. All in all, it was a society most young men felt was worth defending.

The war had one major effect on the country, perhaps not fully appreciated today. The long lines of the unemployed or under employed at the offices dispensing "commodities", that is surplus citrus fruit, cornmeal, potatoes etc., all but disappeared as the more enterprising left for employment in the war industries in Detroit, Wright -Patterson Field and elsewhere.

My high school career ended at the age of seventeen in the summer of 1942 with a "year" of physics compressed into one term of summer school at "U High" in Lexington, three years after I started high school. The war really had little effect on my life at that point. That was probably the case with most civilians not in the war effort or with no family members in service.

College Days in Wartime

> Hark! I hear the tramp of thousands
> And of armed men the hum.
> Lo! A nation's hosts have gathered
> Round the quick alarming drum
> Saying "Come freeman, come
> Ere you're heritage is wasted" said the
> quick alarming drum.
> *Bret Harte*, Reville, st 1

For reasons which are not clear to me the war seemed to have had a moderately minor effect on college life in the fall and early winter term of 1942-43. Students who were in ROTC (Reserve Officer's Training Corps) were apparently deferred, all freshmen and sophomore male students were required to take ROTC so that the draft seemed to have little effect on that group and I believe that juniors and seniors were also deferred if they continued in advanced ROTC. I suspect that there were really not sufficient training facilities built at the time to take care of a massive influx of student age draftees if all able bodied males were called up. Then too, a university career was not regarded at that time as something that everyone could expect to pursue and the college pool of manpower was not relatively as numerous as it is today. The Great Depression was just coming to an end, as a result of the "kick" that defense spending was giving the economy. The knowledge that we were slated for service in the near future was always there and understandably contributed to an air of "Eat, drink and be merry for tomorrow we die" so that scholarship tended at times to have a low priority.

I enrolled in the engineering school at the University of Kentucky and in the Signal Corps ROTC, that being standard for engineering students. At the time there were only about 2500 students on the campus. Undoubtedly some of the junior faculty had been drafted and I have the recollection that most of the faculty were either elderly or, in the humanities, female. We were on the quarter system, expected to attend four quarters comprising the entire year so that graduates could enter the military with a degree somewhat earlier. Classes in general ran from eight A M to five P M and until noon on Saturday. The usual college social activities functioned as before; college football and basketball were continued, though there was less following of the team on road trips due

5

to gas rationing. A steak, salad and baked potato with coffee was seventy-five cents. I think whiskey was being rationed but rum, generally thought to be less desirable, was available. I didn't drink so it made little difference to me. Cigarettes were available but the more popular brands almost disappeared to be replaced by off brands which tasted like sweepings off the factory floor. Transportation was a problem, trains and buses were terribly overcrowded but, on the whole, civilian life was not bad at all! People had money though things to spend it on were growing a bit scarce. The common reply to requests for scarce goods was "Don't you know there is a war on?", often made by a clerk in a store to a soldier in full uniform with campaign ribbons on his chest. The general stress level was moderately elevated, the common excuse for rudeness and lack of consideration, then as now.

Near the end of the winter quarter, 1943, the draft age members of the ROTC got the word that they were to be called into service at the end of March. The president of the University, Dr. Herman Donavan, gave a talk in convocation at that time on "What I See From My Window" in regard to his perception of the course of events in the near future. That night most of the male student body gathered in the dormitory quadrangle and flowed (Well, actually some were lubricated enough to flow) over to the lawn by the president's home, built a bonfire and called to him-"Hey Herman, what do you see now?". It was a bit rowdy but destructive in only a minor way. Some of the football players threw the wooden forms in which wall plaster was being mixed during renovation of a dorm out of the dorm window but no great damage was done. Quite different from the student riots of the Vietnam war era. Everyone expected to go and most went willingly. I understand that a Roper poll in 1939 indicated that only 2.5% of American people were in favor of our entry into the war but Pearl Harbor made all the difference in the world. We now had a clear call and a national leadership dedicated to winning the war, a sharp difference from our leadership during the Vietnam era.

My eighteenth birthday was in April and, like most other young men at that time, I had no desire to remain in school with my classmates away in service. At the end of the quarter in March I quit school and volunteered through the draft, the only way I could do so at that time, for service as soon as possible after my eighteenth birthday. Life with most of my friends gone to war seemed to be a very dull state of affairs.

The drum beat was now distinct.

Uncle Sam Wants You

"Now these are the laws of the jungle
And many and mighty are they
But the head and the hoof and the haunch and
the hump is Obey."

Rudyard Kipling

On June 29th, 1943, the local quota of cannon fodder left the peaceful world of Morgan County for the reception center at Fort Thomas, Kentucky, just south of Cincinnati. Fifteen new citizen soldiers rode the old blue and white bus, following a nice locally sponsored banquet the night before. The juke box in the restaurant played the Andrews Sisters song "I'll Be With You In Apple Blossom Time" and Spike Jones' "Sheik of Araby" as we boarded the bus. Five of us were high school classmates, one of whom was a survivor of the Pearl Harbor attack, having enlisted at the age of sixteen under false pretenses and was discharged shortly after the war began. We had volunteered to enter service on the same date hoping to get to stay together. One went to the Engineers in Fort Belvoir, Virginia, one to the Medical Corps in Washington state, one to the Coast Artillery in California, one to the Air Force in Texas and I went to Camp Fannin, Texas in the Infantry, which was the branch I requested. None of the others got their requested branch or service.

I had taken the examination for ASTP (Army Specialized Training Program) and made a good grade on it. The purpose of the program was to continue accelerated college work for students in fields such as medicine, engineering and other hard sciences in order to maintain those disciplines in our generation. I suppose the experience of the British with their horrendous losses of educated young men in the First World War may have been a factor in setting up the program. All the candidates had to take basic infantry training which had been cut back to thirteen weeks from the previous seventeen weeks. The need for manpower in combat had become acute by that time. The campaigns in the South Pacific and Africa were in full swing.

The Officer Candidate Schools (OCS) for most services of the Army (Quartermaster, Ordnance and other "noncombatant" troops) were back logged and pretty well tapering off with a sufficient current supply of officers. The combat arm (Infantry, Artillery, Engineers, Cavalry or Armor) schools were back logged, though less so, and taking a fair number of enlisted men with combat

7

experience. A score of 110 on the army's placement examination was required for consideration for enrollment in OCS. The average score in my training battalion was over 130, none were below 110. Many had a year or more of college, some had been accepted in medical school or graduate school and most were in good physical condition.

When we got off of the train from Fort Thomas at Camp Fannin in the very early morning it felt like we had stepped into an oven. It was *hot* and it stayed hot until October, days on end with temperatures over one hundred degrees. We trained intensively from about seven in the morning until five in the evening; the usual things: physical education, close order and extended order drill, marksmanship on the M1 rifle, carbine, machine gun, mortar and, that anachronism, the bayonet. There was a battalion review every Saturday evening at five P.M. That was the worst thing of all, worse than the five mile forced march every morning before breakfast. For the review we stood immobile in the hot Texas sun for what seemed hours and men began passing out like clockwork while the "meat wagons," two and a half ton trucks, carried them to the aid station to be treated for heat exhaustion. The treatment consisted of covering them with wet sheets and blowing fanned air across the sheets, there was no air conditioning. One stocky redhead from Alaska passed out regularly on the early morning forced march. He swore that he had never seen the temperature over seventy degrees before coming to Texas.

I was in third platoon, B Company, 48th Training Battalion, 14th Training Regiment. The platoon sergeant, Sgt. Mate, was an ex Marine but was about thirty and found it very difficult to keep up with the young men in the platoon. He had terrible heat rash for which there was no effective treatment. The physical demands were rough, primarily because of the heat, but most of us took it quite well and quickly reached top notch physical condition. The company commander, Lieutenant Miller, was a very macho individual, tall, in rugged physical condition, with a deep bass voice and a military bearing. We all admired him; he was an excellent and inspiring leader but a demanding one. The first sergeant, Sergeant Gilbreath, was a small, wiry, intense and forceful man who got everyone's attention immediately and held it until the training cycle was completed. I still remember them both with great respect.

A major purpose of basic training is to instill a sense of unquestioning discipline and readiness to obey orders. This is probably the most difficult thing for a person who feels that he is of moderate intelligence to accept but experience has shown it to be essential, time after time. People who have never been in service seem unable to comprehend this. Military service in a front line combat unit is probably the only workable form of a truly communistic society where the good of the self is subverted to the good of the group. Our group seemed to have little difficulty in understanding the concept though there were the usual bitches about some things that seemed trivial or arbitrary.

A few things still stand out in my memory from those days of basic training. The last week in the training cycle we bivouacked in the field and marched two hundred and ten miles in seven days, on the way to and from field exercises in the heat of a Texas August. Some "higher up" conceived of the concept of "water discipline" and had the bright idea that young men could get along on an issue of one quart of water a day for all purposes, drinking, shaving etc. He probably was in an air conditioned room in the Pentagon and certainly had not the least conception of fluid and electrolyte balance. While on bivouac we spent our spare moments searching for water, any water. I remember drinking from a spring that emerged from a small cemetery containing recent grave sites. The water was delicious. We were permitted to bathe with water passed in steel helmets from an algae filled pond one night. I'm sure most of us drank at least two helmets full of that water. I suppose someone thought that "water discipline" was a valid idea since we were only issued a quart a day. In actuality we probably needed at least five or six quarts a day in that heat.

Late in the course of the training cycle we began receiving assignments to various colleges for our further education. I found that I was assigned to Texas A & M in engineering. I had two quarters of engineering at the University of Kentucky and found that the ASTP engineering course would start with what was basically first quarter engineering, that I wouldn't pick up where I left off until third quarter in the spring. I had no desire to essentially repeat the work I had done and found that I liked the rough and tumble of life in the infantry so I requested that I be permitted to leave the ASTP program and be assigned to a combat unit. The interviewing officer agreed with my viewpoint, in fact congratulated me on it, and granted my request. He felt we needed soldiers more than students at that time.

I'm probably one of the very few people in service who got the assignment he asked for. Young men think they are immortal. Casualties? That's other people! Not me. The entire combatant military system is based on that premise. In retrospect you might say I was stupid to sign out of a free educational program but that decision probably saved my life. Most of my platoon mates went to Texas A & M and stayed in school until the fall of 1944 when the casualties in the Pacific and Europe precluded the luxury of education of a select group at government expense. They were shipped to Europe as infantry replacements without further training and probably were not in tip top condition. Most were assigned to the 106th or 99th divisions which were green divisions overrun in the German winter offensive of the Bulge (the German Ardennes counteroffensive). I kept up a correspondence with several of them but the letters I mailed after the Bulge began were largely returned marked Killed In Action or Missing. A strange turn of events; I volunteered for combat, I survived and they did not.

I suppose one always remembers those men who were in the first platoon you served with in a special way. As a whole and individually they were fine young men. We had a feeling of cohesion and fellowship; we tended to be very close and enjoyed the singing while on the march. One of the men was a very good accordionist and, in the evenings, the company enjoyed singing along with him and others who played guitars. The little spare time we had, and it was very little, was quite enjoyable. There was little time or facility for organized sports, Uncle Sam needed soldiers, not athletes.

The townspeople in Tyler, the nearest town, were very friendly. We were the first troops in training in Camp Fannin and they were not yet overwhelmed by soldiers. When we could go into town to church after a few weeks of restriction to the base we were invariably invited into people's homes for Sunday dinner.

Camp Shelby

Oh, it's Tommy this and Tommy that
And chuck him out, the brute.
But 'e's the saviour of 'is country
When the guns begin to shoot.

Rudyard Kipling

In early October of 1943 I boarded a train for a slow, peaceful ride through the crimson and gold fall countryside of the deep central South, riding from Camp Fannin, near Tyler, Texas, to Camp Shelby, near Hattiesburg, Mississippi. There I was assigned to Cannon Company, 273rd Infantry Regiment , 69th Infantry Division, for unit training. The 69th division, of course, called itself the Fighting 69th which was a label given the old 69th Infantry Regiment of World War One. During the Second World War that regiment, a National Guard one, was renamed the 165th Infantry Regiment and was part of the 27th Infantry Division which fought in the Pacific island landings. The 69th and the 65th Infantry Divisions, the latter also in Camp Shelby, were both units activated after Pearl Harbor and largely filled by draftees.

As a point of information, an infantry division at that time consisted of three infantry regiments, each consisting of three battalions, each battalion consisting of three rifle companies and a heavy weapons company as well as a battalion headquarters company. The rifle and weapons companies bore most of the brunt of the actual fighting during the World Wars. In addition to the battalion formations each regiment had a Service and Supply Company, an Antitank Company with 57mm antitank guns, a Cannon Company with six 105 mm. short barreled infantry howitzers which provided up close artillery fire to the regiment and a Regimental Headquarters Company.

The Cannon Company had three platoons, each consisting of two 105mm howitzer sections, and a company headquarters platoon. My platoon sergeant, Sgt. Grout, was a rather odd individual, Regular Army with service in the Phillipines and heavily tattooed. He probably did not have a great deal of formal education but knew his business with the guns and, all in all, was pleasant and competent. The platoon leaders were all young men in their mid twenties, of Irish descent and very pleasant. One was named McCabb, another McKee but I can't recall the name of the third lieutenant.

I was assigned as a cannoneer and eventually became first cannoneer in my section. There were six cannoneers, a gunner, and a section leader in each section along with a weapons carrier driver who drove the six wheeled vehicle that pulled the gun, which weighed about 2400 pounds. We had a pleasant outfit with only one misfit who was psychologically unfit for service (actually I think he was paranoid) and eventually he was transferred out. Two of my friends, David Townsend from Boston and Johnny Shultz from Plains, Ohio, were among the most pleasant people I have ever met. The three of us had three day passes to New Orleans together after being picked as the soldiers to represent the company on an honor guard for a new post commandant. They gave us three days in barracks to put the final spit and polish on before serving on the honor guard. As a result we missed several days of bad weather in the field, a nice bonus, and incidentally spent all of our collective funds before dark the first day of our New Orleans pass.The rest of the pass we survived on coffee and doughnuts at the USO, a service organization that provided entertainment for servicemen. A friendly bartender at the Old Absinthe House gave us occasional free drinks so we needed no money.

The fall and winter were spent largely in the field on maneuvers. The 442nd Combat Team, consisting of Nisei troops (Japanese Americans largely from Hawaii and the West Coast) were our usual opponents. They were magnificent soldiers and later became the most decorated regiment in the American armed forces with an outstanding combat record in Italy and France. They felt they had to prove their patriotism and they did, in spades! They were small and looked, from the rear, like a full field pack with legs and a head but had tremendous endurance and morale. However, we saw little of them from the rear; they were usually attacking. On one extended maneuver they were the enemy landing on the Gulf coast and we were the defenders. We"'fought" all through the pine woods of the DeSoto National Forest, from Hattiesburg to Gulfport and Biloxi. On one occasion the 442nd troops broke through the rifle companies' defense line and we had no prime mover to move the gun so we balanced on it with the trails (the two projections toward the rear of the gun which dig in and absorb the recoil) in the air and rode it down one of the few hills in that part of Mississippi and escaped the loss of our gun. Not many people have ridden an artillery piece. It was tricky and not highly recommended for sport.

On another occasion we floated the gun across Lake Shelby on a makeshift raft but lost it in the lake. Luckily we were able to winch it out with a cable on a truck but the water was cold in January, even in the deep South, and dragging a heavy steel cable out in six to eight foot water was no pleasure. The gun was hard to find. The gun had only recently been to Ordnance for a complete breakdown and cleansing, all undone by the "sinking" and we had to spend another night in Ordnance for a complete cleaning and overhaul of the gun. No rest for the wicked!

German POWs (prisoners of war) marched out of their prison camp with picks and shovels on their shoulders like rifles singing "Lili Marlene", "Happy Wanderer" and other classical drinking songs on their way to construction projects on the lake and other areas. Some of them were happy to be out of the war but others were obviously ardent Nazis and would have fought again, given the chance. They all maintained a rather impressive military bearing.

There were local moonshiners in the deep pine woods of south Mississippi who seemed to appear whenever we stopped for a few minutes. The men from the northern cities were fascinated by them but quickly discovered that the local product should be called "Old Headsplitter" (the local term was Panther Piss) as they had some horrendous hangovers. The feral hogs that roamed the pine forest were also a source of interest to them. The hogs were occasionally aggressive, several were shot in "self defense" resulting in some angry local farmers and poor public relations.

Camp Shelby had about 130,000 troops on the post. There were only 20,000 people or so (my guess) in Hattiesburg. On weekends the little town was overwhelmed with bored young men who filled the restaurants and beer joints. Some of the locals understandably resented being crowded out of their familiar haunts and there were a few signs like "Soldiers and dogs stay out," "Coffee five cents, for soldiers ten cents", but for the most part we were treated as well as one might expect under the circumstances. After all, even the British whom we were in England to help, commented that Americans were "Over paid, over fed, over sexed and over here." Understandable, even the best of friends can wear you out. It was a contrast to the town of Tyler, Texas, where we were the first troops and were always welcome.

Frankly, I enjoyed the outdoor life and the camaraderie as much as I have any other period in my life. We were cold and wet on occasion and had the usual gripes about the food, which really wasn't bad under the circumstances of the field kitchens, the mud etc. but we had time to clean up every few days and rest in our pup tents, to read and play softball, volleyball or football with the First Sergeant,"Pop" Johnson, a fat jovial Hawaiian who could place kick a football a mile it seemed, with his bare foot. The football games usually consisted of Captain Wagner being the lone back on one team, "Pop" the lone back on the other team and the rest of the one hundred and thirty or so other men divided into linemen with sixty or so on a side. Great way to rough up your superiors in the mud of the Desoto National Forest!

"Pop" also could take care of the unit's beer consumption quota in grand manner in the PX (post exchange) when we were in the barracks after maneuvers. We usually had a beer party when we came off of maneuvers, consuming a case of beer per man. It was 3.2% beer but it immobilized the company the next day, lots of hangovers.

The barracks themselves were "tropical" barracks, heated with little conical coal stoves, that did little to break the chill of wind whistling through the gaping cracks in the walls. Even KP (kitchen police) when we were on the post wasn't bad, the kitchen was warm and snug but it was disconcerting to see the mess sergeant dip his finger in the food for a taste after slipping his hand inside his pants to scratch his groin, coated with purple gentian violet, the military's standard treatment at that time for jock itch.

In April we heard that all ranks below sergeant were to be shipped overseas as infantry replacements; that the division would fill up with new men out of basic training, undergo unit training again, and than ship overseas. Somehow the word got to one of the men in my company, a Cherokee Indian from Oklahoma who was AWOL (absent without leave), that we were shipping out and he strolled back in dressed in blue jeans and a cowboy hat (during wartime no member of the armed forces was permitted to wear civilian clothes), secure in the knowledge that Uncle Sam needed him at the front, not in the stockade. There was a bit of a scramble by some to claim various disabilities, physical or mental, and some political strings were pulled but that was quite uncommon; most accepted their future without complaint but the drum was beating a good bit louder for most of us. We still knew we were immortal!

So we prepared to leave the 69th Division which later achieved a mild degree of fame by being the first Allied unit to link up with the Russian Army at the Elbe River, deep in Germany. We had another round of inoculations, tetanus, typhus etc., another physical exam (no one was rejected, cannon fodder was in short supply) and turned in old clothing for new.

On the Way

A few days later the trains pulled into Camp Shelby and, to the sound of the divisional band, we boarded the train for Fort Meade, Maryland, between Washington, D.C. and Baltimore. One rather poignant incident occurred in Bristol, Tennessee, when the train stopped for a few minutes and one of the men in our group who was standing in the door of the train, a native of Bristol, saw his fiancee standing there waiting for the train to pass. He jumped off and spent a few minutes with her before we rolled along.

Fort Meade was a staging center for overseas shipment. We had another round of immunizations, my third since entering the service, again ran the infiltration course where troops crawl under machine gun fire aimed about three feet above the ground, repeated small arms qualification and had rather intensive physical education activities.

I was at Fort Meade for three weeks. I had hoped to get a three day pass so I could go home for a farewell visit but was restricted on weekends to a fifty mile radius so that hope was frustrated. My brother Harold, a physician who was due for induction shortly, brought my father, who had suffered several strokes, along with my mother to Washington and I spent a rather sad Sunday with them. Dad commented as they prepared to board the train, "This is probably the last time we will see each other." His health was quite bad, severe hypertension, renal disease and residuals of several strokes and an infantry replacements prospects were not too rosy. The long train ride was quite an ordeal for them. He did make it through the war, I was lucky enough to spend the last seven months of his life at home with him but he died the day my brother Harold got home from Germany , arriving in the evening a few hours after Dad died.

From Fort Meade we were shipped to Camp Shanks, outside of New York City. It was a POE (Port of Embarkation). At least we didn't get any more immunizations! Quite a few of the men were close enough to home to spend the nights or weekends at home. I'm not sure whether it's worse not to get home for a few days before you ship out or to go home every night just before you go. I did spend an afternoon in New York watching the Giants play a ball game at the old Polo Grounds. We had a number of rather good natured brawls in the PX with some nearby paratrooper replacements but most of the few days we had there we were just waiting for the next troop ship. We did a few marches on rural roads in the Hudson Valley area which was lush, green and well trimmed compared to the piney woods of south Mississippi. As I recall we were there

about two weeks. D- Day occurred while we there. It got our attention.
The drum was much easier to hear.

Letter: May 28th-(Camp Shanks) I'm anxious to get overseas and assigned to a regular outfit. I got a rude shock yesterday. A letter I had mailed to Jim Baker, one of my best friends in college, was returned marked KIA (killed in action). He was a B17 navigator and was killed in his second mission over Germany on April 27th, the day we left Camp Shelby.

Don't worry about me, from now on my name is Foxhole Nickell. When better foxholes are built I'll build them.I think I can take care of myself now if I do get into combat and I want to for two reasons. One is that I want to see what it's like and the other is that those who have combat experience will get to come home before the noncombatants.

I'd like to get home for a day or two before shipping out but it seems to be out of the question.

Bon Voyage?

Over there, over there, over there,
We're coming over,
And we won't be back
Till it's over over there.

On the fifteenth of June, exactly one year to the day after I was sworn into the Army, we left Camp Shanks and took the ferry across the New York harbor to the Brooklyn Navy Yard. It was a balmy day and it seemed like an outing, boat ride and all that. There were a number of civilians at the New Jersey terminal who gave us a few well wishes but we were probably old hat to most of them, just another batch of cannon fodder on the way.

We boarded the USS Lejeune, named after the commander of the Second Infantry Division in the First World War, a rather unique unit that had a brigade of infantry (that was two regiments) and a brigade of marines. They wore a huge patch on the left shoulder with an Indian head on it and won fame for their part in the second Battle of the Marne It was a good unit in the Second World War though this time there were no marines in the division. The ship was a converted German passenger liner, the Hamburg, captured off the coast of South America, I understand. It had just been converted to a troopship and this was to be the first transatlantic crossing for most of the crew.

Quarters on board were snug, to say the least. The bunks were pipe racks on which canvas was spread. They were just wide enough to hold a soldier and all of his gear, which was enclosed in a duffel bag. Bunks were stacked about five deep with little vertical space between them. The soldier above me weighed about two hundred and twenty pounds; the bunk sagged and I could slide in on my back but had to get out of bed to turn over, no sleeping on your side. There may have been three feet of aisle space between rows of bunks.

The latrines (heads in naval terminology) were rather unique to our landlubber eyes. There were long troughs through which cold water ran from one end to the other. Two boards about six inches apart, parallel to the troughs and about six inches above the water, ran the length of the troughs and served as seats, a thirty foot long commode of sorts. When the seas were rough and the ship rolled or pitched male genitalia and buttocks were bathed in ice cold sea water. Quiet contemplation was not the order of the day! The showers were cold

17

salt water showers. Salt water soap was issued but little used. One encounter with North Atlantic salt water was more than enough. I suspect the German U boats didn't need radar. They could probably pick us up by the odor.

I don't know how many troops were on board but most were confined to the cabins for most of the day, possibly allowed on deck for an hour or so a day. My company was lucky. We got to pull watch, sitting or standing in raised steel tub like structures for four hours on watch and eight off which gave us eight hours of fresh air (and rain occasionally) a day. I loved it. The convoy was impressive to me, ships almost as far as I could see. We had binoculars and were supposed to scan constantly for submarine periscopes but it was fascinating to watch the ships, especially the destroyers which circled the convoy constantly. The only capital ship with us was, I think, the cruiser Cincinnati. The convoy zig zagged constantly, maximum speed of the convoy was limited to the speed of the slowest vessel and was about six or seven knots.

We had several days of cold rough weather off the coast of Iceland in the "Torpedo Junction" area. Overcoats felt very good, especially at night. As might be expected on the maiden transatlantic trip for the crew we did have one major mishap, The rudder control broke down and we were forced to drop out of the convoy for several hours while repairs were made. It happened on my watch and I thought the rest of the convoy was on a collision course with us as the convoy made a scheduled zig zag turn but our ship failed to respond, continuing straight ahead, nearly colliding with another ship. Lots of Aldis light (lights with shutters which blinked out Morse code) talk back and forth for a while. A destroyer circled us repeatedly while repairs were being made. It happened in daylight, actually there is very little darkness at those latitudes in June, and we intensified our search for periscopes considerably. Never saw one the whole trip.

One advantage of being on watch was the fact that we got three meals a day, other troops only two. Food was served cafeteria style; we ate standing at tables with raised margins to keep the trays from falling off but food did manage to jump the barriers on occasion. Navy food was excellent, they even had ice cream! And milk! And it's true, they serve beans (navy beans, what else?) three times a day. The cooks must have put in very long hours to feed all the troops on that ship. Naval personnel ate in a separate mess. Rumor was that their food was far better but we felt absolutely spoiled after a winter on maneuvers with cold coffee from Jerry cans and cold food from Marmac cans, all designed to keep food and liquids warm but ineffective in cold weather

By and large the trip was uneventful. We had an occasional battle station alert, usually a drill, and occasionally we would hear naval gun fire, just clearing guns and practice firing. It was a far cry from the trip to Iceland that Lt. Murphy, my subsequent company executive officer, had in February of 1942. I understand that over twenty ships in his convoy were sunk in one night. I hate to think of lying packed in the hold of a transport in the dark of a North Atlantic winter night and hearing the torpedo hits and ships breaking up. Are we next? The U-boat wolf packs were in full hue and cry then. I understand that in 1945 95% of the U boats that went to sea never returned. Horrible way to die!

On June 29th, a year from the day I went on active duty, we entered the Irish Channel from the north, passing the Mull of Kintyre and Arran Island. Scotland and Ireland appeared incredibly green. Scotland, in particular was beautiful in the bright sunlight with red tiled roofs and green hills. The channel was busy with large and small commercial and military shipping constantly in sight. The seas were calm and the day pleasant. We anchored in the Greenock harbor area and disembarked into lighters or small ferry like craft. I attempted to talk to one of the local seamen but his brogue was such that I couldn't understand anything he said except "Aye, Mate."

We boarded trains, travelling through Glasgow which seemed depressing, slums, shipyards, heavy industry and all that. The train continued on through Edinburg which seemed much cleaner and prettier with wider streets and more greenery. The train ran down the east coast of England, passing a number of airfields with British Stirling and Lancaster bombers taking off for night missions over Europe. The British compartments on the trains were strange to us. The excitement of the moment was enough to keep us awake but I did doze off sometime in that short Northern night only to awaken when the train stopped in a barely illuminated long shed like station. I opened the compartment door and asked a man, dimly seen under the light, "How far is it to London?" His reply, "You're in it, Laddy". That was my sole experience in the capitol of the great British Empire.

The train continued on to Camp Heathcliffe, near Honiton, England, not far from Exeter. The countryside was not heavily populated in the area of the camp. I suspect it was in the Dartmouth Moors Park in view of the nature of the countryside and the name of the camp though I can't locate Honiton on my maps. The camp was rather primitive, box like temporary barracks, with mummy shaped straw filled mattresses laid on wooden frames strung with chicken wire for beds. We had two meals a day, tea and cold oatmeal for breakfast and cold potatoes, rutabaga and cold fish or mutton in the evening. Fish and chips could be purchased in the NAAFI (Navy, Army, Air Force Institute, much like our USO i.e. United Service Organization, both of which provided a sparse club like setting for off duty troops). The British beer was warm and undrinkable to my adolescent taste. We were permitted to go into the local village but there was little to see there. The beer was cheaper at the NAFI and there was little to choose from in the way of food, aside from fish and chips (fried potatoes), also available at the NAAFI.

We were in the Second Replacement Battalion which was just what the name implies, a source of replacements for casualties occurring in Normandy. Training was not too strenuous. We hiked about the countryside every day, usually in light drizzle, and sighted in weapons. "Night problems" were run in daylight as it didn't get dark until eleven or so at night, Britain being on double daylight saving time. All in all it was a rather restful period. We tried to keep up with events in Normandy but had little access to news other than brief bulletins posted on the company bulletin board. Little did we know that, once we were committed to combat, we would know nothing about the campaign except what we could see with the naked eye from our current position. There is no condition in human existence more chaotic and disorganized than a battlefield. We were not far from several British airfields and there was a great deal of aerial traffic, especially at night or late evening. Several bombers crashed in the area of the camp, returning from missions over the Continent.

On July 16th we loaded up on trucks and drove through the English countryside to the embarkation port of Plymouth. The fields in the area were packed with military supplies, trucks, jeeps, tanks, ammunition dumps and boxes of military gear, mind boggling to observe. The air overhead was crowded with American B-17, B-26 and B-25 bombers, P-47 and P-51 fighter planes and the most famous planes of the Second World War, British Spitfires with their beautiful lines and great maneuverability. Tethered blimps, which were large ballons held by heavy wire cables, floated overhead to ward off low level aerial attacks. A common joke was that there was so much military equipment in southern England the blimps were needed to keep the island from sinking.

We left the trucks at the top of a hill and hiked down in the twilight a few hundred yards through the streets of Plymouth to the harbor and embarked in LCIs (Landing Craft Infantry), then were carried out to the HMS Cheshire which lay at anchor in Plymouth Bay. It was a real rust bucket, beat up, small and filthy dirty. Our crew consisted primarily of Indian civilians. Quarters for my company were in the mess area, hammocks were slung over the tables after a meal of cold broiled fish and potatoes was eaten. The meal was not notably appealing and was less so in retrospect when we watched the cooks stand in the large cooking trays in their bare feet and scrub them out with a broom and no soap.

Letter; June 30th-As you can see I'm in England and I must say it's certainly beautiful here. The fields are well kept with stone walls or hedges around them and the homes are nice, some with thatched roofs. The English people are friendlier than I thought they'd be.

Letter: Date ?-Still in England-Blaine, I'm pretty sure I'll get back OK but will you get the telephone office to notify you before they do Mom and Dad if anything should happen to me. I'm not worried about myself but anything can happen.

Normandy

Fair stood the wind for France
When we our sails advance;
Nor now to prove our chance
Longer will tarry;
But putting to the main, at Caux, the mouth of the Seine,
with all his martial train
Landed King Harry.

Agincourt- Michael Drayton

Well, actually King Harry wasn't with us this time. In spirit maybe, but not in body. He probably would have loved it!

Johnny Shust and I spent the night on deck as we watched the English coast fade in the distance and ships in the convoy move slowly toward the Normandy coast. It seemed high adventure to us as the destroyers circled through the area in a search for submarines and an even greater thrill when, about one PM in the afternoon of July 17th, we began to make out a low lying haze which was the Normandy coast. The Channel was filled with ships moving toward and away from the coast. As we approached the shore we could see several large naval vessels, battleships and cruisers, lying close in and shelling targets inland. The beachhead extended only a few miles inland, even 42 days after the initial landing. There was constant overhead activity, mostly fighter planes and medium bombers en route to attack positions in the bocage (the Norman hedgerow country).

We went over the side on landing nets, carrying our weapons and duffel bags, loading into landing craft twenty or thirty feet below the deck of the ship. It was a bit scary as the swells would lift the landing craft five or six feet and it would swing away from the side of the ship, several feet occasionally. The sea was relatively calm, moderate breeze blowing and the weather was sunny, cool and beautiful. Our LCI landed us on Utah Beach at seven PM.

The original landing there had been made by the Fourth Infantry Division with less opposition than that encountered by the First and Twenty- Ninth Divisions at Omaha Beach. The beach was a beehive of activity with troops and supplies being unloaded. The area behind the beach was flat except for sand dunes, perhaps twenty feet or so in height. The quartermaster troops handling supplies had made rather elaborate dugouts, scattered through the dunes, from shipping crates.

Letter-France, about July 20th-I'm fine and satisfied though I'll be happier when I'm assigned to a regular unit again. I hope to get in the censored, censored, censored (all mail was read by one of the officers and unit names or places could not be stated directly), *it's an honor to be in one of those outfits.*

The exit from the beach passed by a German concrete bunker through a gap in the dunes and through some flat swampy land into the hedge row country. In the 1980s we went back to Utah beach to see a very peaceful looking scene with a young man riding a sail board on wheels up and down the beach. The block house is the only sign of former events.

Replacement Depots in Hedgerow Country

No great dependence is to be placed on the eagerness of young
soldiers for action, for the prospect of fighting is agreeable
to those who are strangers to it.
Vigetius- Roman military writer, 4th century, A.D.

We marched inland for a few miles, passing through small villages which were rather heavily damaged by shell fire, and bivouacked in an apple orchard. American fighter planes stopped most of their activity about ten PM and the Luftwaffe began flying over, dropping bombs in the beach area. The air seemed filled with antiaircraft fire, tracers from 50 caliber machine guns drew red lines all over the sky. It was the most spectacular fireworks show ever seen, repeated every night. I think the reason our fighters stopped flying was due to the fact that we had so much antiaircraft capability. The Luftwaffe was also relatively weak at that time. Any American planes flying at night were apt to be hit by friendly fire.

We dug slit trenches next to the hedgerows which were such a formidable obstacle to our troops' advancement in Normandy. These were not "hedgerows" in the sense we Americans think of them, privet hedge, box woods or bois d' arc. They were stone walls erected hundreds of years ago as the rocky fields of Normandy were cleared for cultivation. Over the years they had become overgrown with vines, trees had grown up on them and they were often three feet or more in thickness and six feet or more high. The enclosed fields varied in size,many were no more than a hundred to two hundred feet wide so that there was a new "fortress" every few hundred feet. The Germans dug deep standing depth foxholes behind the hedgerows and punched holes in the base of the hedgerow to permit a good field of fire for the machine guns which they relied on so heavily. They had also placed vertical posts called "Rommel's asparagus" in the larger fields as obstacles to glider landings. We commandeered the poles and used them as volleyball net supports, playing around crashed gliders. The second day we were there two ME-109s strafed the field. They caused only one or two casualties and we had the satisfaction of seeing three Spitfires jump them immediately and shoot them down.

On the 19th we were moved to a forward replacement depot. That night

I was on guard, standing next to a hedgerow during a strafing and bombing raid which caused about 30 casualties in nearby fields. Jerry didn't have to be very accurate with his bombing as every field was filled with men and material. A dud 90 mm. antiaircraft shell fell just across the hedgerow from me, gave me a bit of a start. I'm sure we had quite a few casualties from spent bullets and shrapnel from the anti aircraft fire, there was so much of it.

On the 20th of July Don Seely, one of my closer friends, was assigned to the 83rd Division. Don was a real gungho soldier who wanted very badly to be assigned to a regular army unit but the 83rd had a good combat record. I never heard from Don again.

On the 22nd a large consignment, was made; this time to the 5th Division. They called almost all of the men I had shipped with but skipped Johnny Shust's name and assigned him to the 2nd Division. Dave Townsend went to the 1st Division. I really hated to be separated from those two, we had such good times together in Camp Shelby. Johnny made it through the war, I don't know if Dave did.

Then we loaded into trucks and were driven to the 5th Division Replacement Depot, passing several airfields with their woven metal landing strips, which were constantly busy with P-47s landing, refueling and taking off. We noted some Negro troops along the road wearing gas masks, which caused a moderate degree of consternation. Shortly thereafter we noted a long line of two and a half ton trucks filled with dead American soldiers stacked in like cord wood. They were being unloaded at a military cemetery, placed in white GI mattress covers and buried in graves being dug by German POWs (prisoners of war). There seemed to be several hundred waiting to be buried. It had been a very exciting time, disembarking in Normandy, watching the aerial side show, passing artillery firing missions against the enemy, and observing the massive troop buildup. We were in high spirits until we saw the dead American soldiers and smelled the unique stench of decaying human flesh. Perhaps the most surprising thing was the fact that so many of the dead had turned black in the process of decay; not just the livor mortis of blood seeking a dependent position after death, which is a purple discoloration, but a definite black color. Laughing and light hearted joking came to a screeching halt. At that point we realized that war was something besides rationing, headlines and brass bands.

Many fields contained dead Norman cattle, black and white, with their distinctive black "spectacles" surrounding their eyes, killed by artillery fire. They were massively distended with their legs displaced laterally by intestinal gas. Evidence of death, human and animal, was not hard to find.

We were in First Army area, the only American army in Normandy at that time. I understand that Patton issued an order, after Third Army became active in France, that replacements would not be driven by active military cemeteries. When we arrived at the 5th Division Replacement Depot we dug in not over 300 yards from the division's GRO (Graves Registration Office) where, every day, truckloads of 5th division dead were processed. Not too good for replacement morale.

Shortly after our arrival a German ME -109 fighter plane carried out a strafing run while a Red Cross van was serving coffee and doughnuts, needless to say it interrupted the serving line. No casualties. This was while we were in the Cerisy Forest, a short distance from the front at the time. There were artillery units around us and we occasionally received a few rounds of counter battery fire.

There was a mixture of all sorts of units in our immediate area, American, British and Canadian. One of the men in a Canadian engineer unit near us expressed the usual jealousy other armies had for relatively highly paid Americans. His pungent remark about being on British rations was "They don't even give us any bloody arse wipe". After the war I found that Canada had conscription but only volunteers were sent overseas until late in the war. The Canadian troops in combat strongly resented the riots that occurred in the nonvolunteering troops and were none too happy with their pay, British Army rations etc.

While we were in the replacement depot, Repo Depo as it was called, we were taken to a shower point, that is showers in field tents, and while we were there we watched the bombing runs on the St. Lo area. St. Lo had been a particularly tough objective. It was decided to try pattern bombing of the area to "soften the Germans up." The first planes over were fighter bombers, then B-25s and B-26s, which attacked the German antiaircraft guns as well as targets of opportunity. Then the earth began to vibrate as heavy bombers, B-17s and B-24s, began to arrive. The Stars and Stripes, the newspaper of the invasion army, said there were three thousand bombers. They seemed to come in an endless stream; the noise of the bombs falling about five miles from us was continuous. On that occasion the wind at ground level was blowing from the German to the American lines. The initial bomb strikes were on target but later bombs were aimed at the smoke line from earlier bombing and the bombs fell on American troops who had been pulled back a mile or so to avoid such a problem, killing the commander of all American ground forces, Lt. General McNair, as well as a number of other Americans. None-the-less, the subsequent ground attack went forward successfully, beginning the "breakout" through the St. Lo area which broke up the impasse of the Normandy campaign and allowing the following sweep across Northern France.

There has been a great hue and cry about "friendly fire" deaths following the few incidents in the Gulf War and a lieutenant colonel has been forced to resign his commission as a consequence of one of them. They were quite common in the Second World War and probably in every war fought. The American Navy shot down almost half of the airborne force flying over them in the Sicilian invasion. It is sheer nonsense to think that, under conditions of poor visibility and the stress of combat, they are avoidable. Our news media, whose commentators make daily egregious mistakes and terribly poor predictions, commit a grave error in suggesting that these episodes could be avoided.

Second Infantry Regimental Insignia

29

Able Company

Then out spake brave Horatius,
The Captain of the Gate
"To everyman upon this earth
Death comes soon or late.
And how can man die better
Than facing fearful odds
For the ashes of his fathers
and the temples of his Gods."

Horatius at the Bridge-*Macaulay*

The next evening they moved us up to join our companies. We spent the night in a recently harvested wheat field, the yellow straw in colorful contrast to the lush green of the hedgerow foliage. We were the first contingent of combat replacements that the 5th Division had received. An officer began calling names of the replacements and assigning them to various companies. He called off a long list of names to go to Able (phonetic spelling for A at that time) Company. I thought "I don't want to go to a company that gets thrown in hot places like that.." Then they skipped down and began assignments to M (Mike) company. I thought I might be assigned there but they called "Nickell, Able Company." I wouldn't have given a plugged nickel for my chance of making it through the war at that time. As it turned out I became a plugged Nickell.

I was assigned to the weapons platoon, which consisted of a machine gun section made up of two light .30 caliber machine gun squads of five men each, a section leader and runner, and a 60 mm. mortar section, made up of three squads of five men, a section leader and a runner. It seems that my experience as a gunner on a 105 mm. howitzer gave me the experience to understand the use of indirect fire (that is, firing at objectives that can't be directly visualized by the gunners). I was assigned to the 3rd mortar squad.

Lt. King was a new company commander. He had been assigned to A Company, leaving his old position as executive officer in C or Charlie Company, replacing Captain Schmidt who had been wounded in the first day of the Vidouville attack, part of the attack to clear Highway 3 linking the German lines from Caen to St. Lo. Captain Schmidt stayed with the company for five days after he was wounded leading the attack which cleared the village, and received the Distinguished Service Cross, the second highest military decoration, for personal heroism above the call of duty.

Lieutenant Murphy was the company executive officer. He lasted longer than any officer in the company, surviving until the Ardennes campaign, quite exceptional. Most of our officers were killed or wounded in a matter of weeks. Lt. Murphy was a brave, cool soldier and a compassionate man. I remember him with great respect.

Lt. "Lucky" Ives was the 1st platoon leader, Lt. Darrel, 2nd platoon, Lt. Russell, 3rd platoon and Lt. Myers the weapons platoon leader. Technical sergeant Lawrence Pierce was the platoon sergeant, an outstanding soldier who was one of the few I knew who seemed to enjoy many aspects of combat. Sgt. Ramicone was mortar section leader and Hank Terzago the section runner.

First mortar squad consisted of Sgt. Coty, squad leader (and incidental interpreter of French for the company); Judge, gunner; Novac, assistant gunner; Halloran and Murray,(a replacement for Frank Brickman who was wounded and later rejoined the company) ammunition bearers.

Second mortar squad consisted of Sgt. Herman Heath, squad leader; Orville Chaney, gunner; Rosenow, assistant gunner; Pryzdraga and Miller, (both replacements for men wounded or killed at Vidouville) ammunition bearers.

Third squad consisted of Sgt. "Trigger" Twargowsky, a fine no nonsense soldier, squad leader; George O'Conner, a gunner who had received the Silver Star for picking off snipers at Vidouville, Andy Carpenter, assistant gunner and Joe Capp and I were ammo bearers. I replaced a very popular man who had been killed in the division's first attack.

I found that Chaney and I, as well as a Cassidy boy in the third platoon, were all from Morgan County, Kentucky, which statistically seems unlikely as it is a small county but I felt a bit more "at home." Andy Carpenter was from nearby Mt. Sterling, Kentucky, and seemed like "home folks." A replacement in a rifle company really has a rather difficult time in being accepted. A Company had been overseas for over two and a half years and the men felt much like a family. A replacement who took the place of a good friend who had been killed was somewhat resented, even though the new man represented new help in winning the war.

The Second Infantry Regiment, commanded by Colonel Rolfe, was organized in 1798, had been on active duty ever since and was the second oldest regiment in the United States Army. It had seen action in every war the US had ever fought, with the exception of World War One when it was on duty in the Phillipines.

The Fifth Infantry Division was composed of the 2nd, 10th and 11th Infantry Regiments, the 19th, 21st, 46th, and 50th Field Artillery Battalions, 7th Combat Engineer Battalion, 5th Medical Battalion, 5th Signal Company, 5th

Quartermaster Company, 5th Military Police Platoon, and the 5th Ordnance Company. The 735th Tank Battalion and the 818th Tank Destroyer Battalion were attached to, but not an integral part of, the division. The division was the first American division to go to the European Theatre in World War Two, arriving in September and October, 1941. At the time I joined the division we were in the Fifth Corps, First Army, which had made the D-Day landings. The division had made its initial assault at Vidouville on the left flank of the First Army, adjacent to the British, in a drive to secure Highway Three as a supporting maneuver in the assault on St. Lo, preliminary to the breakout on the right flank of First Army at Coutances. They had been relieved by the British and shifted to the west to be the first infantry division out of the Normandy beachhead in the drive to encircle the German armies in Normandy.

The bocage or hedge row country of Normandy was ideal for defense and prohibited effective mobility by the armored or mechanized divisions. Fighting in Normandy was largely infantry combat, gains were daily measured in yards and it was a war of attrition. All in all, it probably was as bitter and bloody as anything American troops encountered in the war.

Breakthrough

St. Lo had fallen to the 29th Division and we were trucked through the remains of the city. It was completely demolished. Few stones remained in contact with one another in their original form. Bulldozers scraped a way through the remains of the town to allow traffic but there were very few remaining citizens. As a result of the bitter fighting a great deal of Normandy was badly damaged and the local people were not always friendly, indeed occasionally openly hostile to Allied troops. As dark approached, we passed through Avranches on the base of the Cotentin peninsula of Normandy, following the 4th and 7th Armored divisions. There was a monumental traffic jam as the entire Third Army, activated under Patton who was now our commander, funneled through the city. We were the first infantry division to break out of Normandy. The corridor at the time was quite narrow and was almost cut by a massive German counterattack at Mortain shortly thereafter but the 30th Division held it open and the counterattack failed.

Once free of the hedgerow country, mounted on trucks and tanks, we moved rather rapidly with little opposition across the base of the Brittany peninsula, roughly following the course of the 4th, 6th and 7th Armored Divisions. There were occasional planned roadblocks which were usually held for a short time before the enemy withdrew but the fighting was rather swift and vicious for a few minutes to a few hours before they left. The armored divisions often just bypassed the areas of resistance as the ground was dry and the terrain ideal for armored movement, leaving the enemy in place for the infantry to take care of as we opened the roads up for supply columns. Most often the enemy was just taken by surprise, unaware that we had penetrated so deeply. In those circumstances they often surrendered with little resistance. In general it was "Cowboy and Indian" fighting with long stretches of unopposed advances, forty or fifty miles a day with little opposition and then a brief violent episode with the men in the lead vehicles often casualties of a mine explosion or an eighty-eight shell.

Usually the advance was led by an armored car, a fast, lightly armored six wheeled vehicle which could move rapidly either forward or backward, the latter for good reason. They could "do a 180" without turning around. They were designed for reconnaisance and not for fighting though they were armed with a machine gun and a 37 mm. cannon. Occasionally a light tank or a jeep led the way. The light tank was really only effective against infantry. The 37 mm.

cannon it carried was totally ineffective against German armored vehicles. The jeep was a small, open four wheel drive vehicle, armed only with a thirty or fifty caliber machine gun, totally devoid of armor. Usually there were two "lead" vehicles which leap frogged one another from time to time so that one did not always bear the burden of the "point" which was exceptionally vulnerable. An infantry platoon attacking in column formation, that is with one or two files with men in line behind one another as opposed to an attack with the men all in line across the axis of attack, also adopted this leapfrog advance of the point men who were the most vulnerable men in the platoon.

Here we began to encounter the FFI (Free French of the Interior) who sometimes could warn us of roadblocks or enemy troop locations. They were usually armed with Sten guns, which were small submachine guns of British origin, presumably parachuted in. Most wore a small armband of red, white and blue and a beret, They were usually quite happy to see us. They were most helpful in giving directions or telling us of enemy troop concentrations but they didn't stay around when there was enemy fire. Frankly, I don't blame them. They weren't well armed or trained and were not very accurate in their estimates of enemy numbers. Their usual response to the question "How many Germans are there?" was "Beaucoup" (many) which might mean five or five hundred. However some of our troops were guilty of the same inaccuracy. One thing the French always did was mooch cigarettes and candy. The children were especially good in soliciting candy. The children's English was limited pretty well to "Cigarette for Papa, Chocolate for Mama" and it usually worked. We were issued a carton of cigarettes a week and there were twelve cigarettes in a day's K rations as well as a chocolate bar so we usually responded to their pleas. American soldiers were notorious for giving away rations.

The response of the civilian population to "liberation" was overwhelming. Many of the villages literally exploded when they realized that the "Boche", as they called the Germans, were gone. There were often French and American flags displayed. We were plied with bottles and glasses of wine as we marched through the towns. They would put a glass of wine in our hands and, as we marched along and finished it, we would exchange the empty glass for a full one. Luckily most of the towns were small ones, the streets weren't long enough for many glass exchanges so we were not incapacitated by the wines. I was a callow and unsophisticated nineteen year old at the time so I didn't care a great deal for wine anyway. None of us were connoisseurs of wine and most of the men preferred the Calvados of Normandy or the Cognac of Brittany to wine, more jolt to the ounce.

Wine bottles rolling about in the floor of the trucks we rode in soon became a hazard as we stumbled over them as we mounted or dismounted the vehicles.The weather was warm, we were in woolen olive drab uniforms and the days were uncomfortable when we dismounted and marched any distance. On one occasion one of the men in the machine gun section, George Odishoo, a short, stocky soldier, passed out from a combination of heat, marching and wine. We were moving pretty fast and left George lying by the roadside. When he awoke he was surprised to find French girls throwing flowers on him. They thought he was dead!

The French made an occasional similar mistake in regard to our latrines. When we were in a stable position we dug a slit trench, usualy about six feet long and two feet or so deep, to use as a latrine. When we left we filled it in and put up a sign labelled "Old Latrine, Company A" and the date. Some of the civilians thought it was a a a grave of an American soldier and put flowers on it. If they had planted flowers on the latrines they would have been well fertilized.

Most everyone received their quota of kisses as we marched through the towns but I'm sure the men in the headquarters companies who followed us received feminine favors which the line companies could not enjoy. Headquarters stayed in the towns, the line companies formed defensive lines on the outskirts of the towns. So be it. All in all, it was a moving experience to enter a French town, see the French and American flags break out and to hear the people spontaneously sing the Marseillaise, call "Vive la Amerique" as we appeared and to see the children march along beside us, usually begging effectively for chocolate.

Movement was generally rapid, troop positions were often confused and we frequently "ran off our maps", with the only guides to our position at the time the local FFI and other civilians.

As we cut across the base of the Brittany peninsula German troops were assigned to hold the major ports of Brest, St. Malo, Nantes and St. Nazaire to prevent their use as ports for Allied supplies. The 10th and 11th Infantry attacked and occupied the cities of Nantes and Angers and the 2nd Infantry, my regiment, set up road blocks between St. Nazaire and Nantes. St.Nazaire was a major submarine base with heavily fortified submarine "pens" and quite a few German marines. There were no definite "lines" at the time. We had German antaircraft positions on all four sides of us when the first and weapons platoon of A company set up a road block in the little village of Sautron 10 km. west of Nantes.

There are some hedgerows in the Brittany area which define the fields and we dug in in vineyards on the west side of the town and awaited events, with machine guns covering the road and an armored car in support of us. Shortly after we dug in two German staff cars came down the road and were met with rifle fire and grenades, killing seven Germans, two were taken prisoner. Shortly thereafter five more Germans were killed at the road block. They had been totally unaware that we were in the vicinity and had just stumbled into our position, just as we stumbled into their roadblock ambushes. Not exactly a chivalric way to fight a war but an effective one, as lethal for one side as the other. They had the advantage most times as we were advancing, they retreating

Shortly thereafter Lt. Myers told us that the Germans were expected to attack us in force in order to clear the road. We moved down the road into another vineyard next to a village and waited for Jerry. A German patrol set fire to a barn nearby, hoping to draw us into the fire light, but we sat tight. The people in the village wanted us to put the fire out but it was an obvious trap.

Joe Capp and I took turns on guard, the usual combat routine of two hours on, two hours off watch. I was next to the hedgerow where another joined it, making a "T". After night fell I heard someone cough near a barn a few hundred feet away where I knew there were no friendly troops. Shortly thereafter I heard something moving along the hedgerow at right angles to the one I was behind. I watched the area closely and soon saw something black, which I took to be a German scuttle bucket helmet, slipping toward me. I aimed my carbine, which was an ammo bearer's standard weapon, at it and fired five rounds. Trigger, my squad leader, slipped down to my position and asked me what I was firing at. I told him I thought I had shot a German. Much to my chagrin I found, when morning came, that my "German" was a chicken, now a casualty of the war, and I was, needless to say, embarrassed. Luckily no one nicknamed me "Chicken Killer."

About eight the next morning a motorcycle carrying two Germans came down the road and met a barrage of small arms fire and the end of the war for them. Six others were following them on bicycles but were trailing a good distance behind the motorcycle and escaped. Just before dusk a German truck came by with soldiers in it and we killed or captured all eight of them.

I was eating a K ration about the time it came and my foxhole buddy with whom I alternated guard duty , a Mexican named Pedilla, dug into a bumble bee's nest and exclaimed "Leeson, Shurman bombers", when he heard the bees buzzing around his head. We were becoming more nervous about our exposed positions as our P47 fighter bombers were bombing and strafing enemy positions on all four directions around us.

Early the next morning a German patrol entered a farmhouse just across a small field from us and roughed up some civilians, killing a woman in the house. That evening we were told that there were fifteen enemy marines a short distance away who wanted to surrender. We sent a patrol down and brought them back in without incident but shortly after dark the Germans came back to the nearby farmhouse, where we could clearly distinguish their guttural speech from that of the French.

The next morning we were told to move out as a strong force of enemy troops was seen advancing on us. We were trucked to Angers which had been captured by the 10th Infantry while we were in Soutron. We were there for two days, getting cleaned up and getting a little rest, bivouacked on the outskirts of the city and generally being treated like royalty by the citizens. I thought it was the most pleasant of all the French towns we entered. The 80th Division then relieved us and we headed north toward Paris.

During this period while we were on the road block someone dug into the content of one of the captured vehicles and discovered a German Army payroll with lots of Belgian francs, mostly in thousand franc notes. We were being paid in occupation army French francs and had no idea what the Belgian money was worth. Most of us ignored it or used it for toilet paper. One of the men, a farsighted one, collected a bag full of the money and sent it to the kitchen to be put in his bed roll. Later, we were paid on one occasion in Belgies (Belgian francs) and he found that he was rather well to do, several hundred (or thousand?) dollars better off than the rest of us. Sad to say, I did not have his foresight.

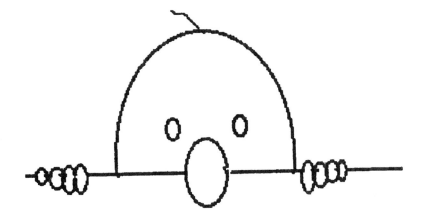

Kilroy was here.
This rather silly little picture greeted troops all over the battlefields of Europe. It was painted on walls, fences, knocked out tanks and every conceivable place, the implication being "Where have you been?" or "What took you so long?"

Life On The Run

I might insert a few words here in regard to how we lived under mobile conditions, riding trucks or tanks in the "Cowboy and Indian" days of hot pursuit across northern France as the Germans fell back into eastern France, Belgium and Holland.

Our uniforms were woolen ODs (olive drab), hot during the day, especially when we were marching, but comfortable at night when a field jacket often felt good. As an ammunition bearer I carried a wooden packboard which contained a "clover leaf" of 60 mm. mortar shells. This consisted of three tubes in clover leaf arrangement, each tube containing six rounds or shells, each weighing three pounds, fifty- four pounds not counting the weight of the packboard. I also carried a raincoat folded over my belt with half of a GI blanket, a canteen, a shelter half (half of a pup tent), an entrenching tool which was sort of a combination shovel and pick modeled on one the German Army had developed, three K rations stuck anywhere I could stick them, a canteen and a first aid pack. In addition I carried a .30 caliber carbine and three to five clips of ammunition. On occasion I also carried a .45 caliber Colt automatic pistol which was not authorized for an ammunition bearer. The latter I took from a gunner, who was authorized to carry the .45, whenever one of them was killed or wounded. All in all, fully laden for combat, I probably carried about 70 pounds in a combat situation. Needless to say, the weight slowed me down a good bit when I attempted to run under fire, the packboard bouncing against my neck with each step. As a rule, when we were in immediate contact with the enemy, we attempted to shed every ounce of excess weight until the fire fight was over and then picked up the essentials for immediate survival.

This did not include the weight of the helmet which was in two parts, the liner which was made of plastic and had internal straps adjustable to our head size, and the external steel helmet which was an all purpose affair. We wore it for protection, used it as a washbasin, drank from it, could boil water or cook in it, though rarely did so and, if pinned down in a foxhole, use it as a urinal. We did not, as usually depicted in movies, wear the helmet chin strap buckled as it was thought that the concussion from a nearby shell or mine exploding could catch the helmet and break your neck. The chin strap on the liner was worn fastened around the back of our heads which kept it on while we ran and was more comfortable than the helmet chin strap.

The assistant gunner in a mortar squad carried the same burden essentially.

The gunner carried the 60 mm. mortar, which weighed 42 pounds, but no packboard. He had the luxury of carrying a combat pack, an expandable knapsack which gave personal gear he carried a little more protection from the weather. As a sidearm he carried a .45 caliber Colt pistol. The ammunition bearers in the machine gun section carried two metal cases containing .30 caliber ammunition loaded into belts, which were of heavy cloth that gave rise to frequent jamming of the gun. The German machine gun belts were made of metal links and their belts and their light machine guns were far superior to ours. The assistant gunner carried the tripod the light machine guns were mounted on, while the gunner carried the machine gun itself. Someone in the squad usually carried spare barrels for the machine gun. The members of the machine gun section were able to wear combat packs, the mortar section was the only one carrying packboards. All of the machine gun section men carried carbines with the exception of the gunner who wore a Colt .45 pistol.

The men in the three rifle platoons carried a Garand M1 .30 caliber rifle which, weighed about eight pounds, was semiautomatic, firing clips of eight rounds before reloading. The rifle squads also had a BAR (Browning automatic rifle) team which consisted of the BAR gunner and three support riflemen who carried extra ammunition pouches in addition to being armed with an M1. The BAR could fire 350 or 600 rounds/minute in the automatic mode; some models could operate in the semiautomatic mode.

During the mobile periods the packboard was in the floor of a truck or on a tank but we had to dismount frequently. There often would be a shuttle, wherein the vehicles would carry men a few miles forward, unload and go back to pick up another load of troops, take them forward to the position of the first load who had been marching forward and repeat the process. Needless to say the shuttle only worked when we were moving with little opposition. On some days in the drive across France we had no vehicles and would march, though rarely more than 15-20 miles a day. With a full combat load and in the heat of August that was enough.

Sleep came easily, though we were never allowed more than two hours at a time; usually half the squad would pull watch for two hours, then the other half would watch for two hours, alternating through the night. We used the raincoat and shelter half as bedclothes, I can't recall ever pitching a tent in the usual manner; we didn't carry tent pegs and couldn't have pitched a tent if we wanted to. When we slept in the rain we put the shelter half under us and the rain coat and half blanket over us and were usually soaked in short order. We slept on the ground and quickly learned that scooping out a shallow hollow for your hips reduces the discomfort of the hard ground, at least a little. We usually dug a shallow slit trench to sleep in whenever possible; surprise encounters with the enemy at night were common and a hole only a couple of feet deep was good protection against small arms fire and hand grenades as well as artillery fire. We dug in singly if the weather was good, two together for warmth if it was cold. When I got home someone asked how far back we had to go to the barracks at night. Of course we never went to a barracks and were rarely in buildings of any sort unless we were street fighting and the buildings in that situation were seldom intact.

We each had a bedroll which was kept in a truck with the company rear headquarters, rarely accessible to us. This contained a spare uniform, underclothes, spare shoes, blankets, personal goods and toilet articles. Most of us carried a toothbrush but no other articles of personal hygiene. When the weather was a little cooler we wore a towel as a scarf and then had something to dry our hands or face with. Few of us shaved when in the mobile front line position though we often did when in a static or nonmobile position. We rarely got to change uniforms or underclothing except when the headquarters trucks were available. We did bathe and do a minimal laundry on rare occasions when we could do so in streams or at a well but I suspect we were a ripe smelling group of young men most of the time.

Our meals when we were on the move consisted of K rations. Breakfast consisted of a small can of eggs and ham, "dog biscuit" which were stony hard canned crackers, a prune bar, powdered coffee, sugar and creamer. Lunch contained canned cheese, thought to be constipating and referred to as "hinderbinder," powdered lemonade which everyone hated but which gave us some vitamin C, and a stony hard chocolate which I'm sure broke a lot of teeth. Supper contained a sort of potted meat and bouillon. They all had four cigarettes of rare and unknown brands. Each ration was wrapped in a cardboard layer and a layer of heavy waterproof waxed paper. The paper could be burned and was enough to heat up a canteen cup of water for coffee or bouillon.

If conditions were favorable, no enemy in close proximity etc., the kitchen would set up and cook a hot meal for us. They tried to send up hot foods in insulated Marmac containers if we were in a stable position but the kitchen could not be close enough for us to go to form a chow line. Carrying parties would go back and carry up food and coffee in Jerry cans as well as ammunition etc. but the coffee was almost always cold and heavily flavored with chlorine, being made with water from water points set up by the Army engineers. We usually preferred to make our own coffee if possible. Food in the Marmac cans was usually also rather cold but a welcome relief from K rations.

There was a ration called a "10 in 1" which was a large carton that contained enough food for ten men for one meal. Unfortunately it was bulky and not suited for infantry to carry and we rarely had it but regarded it as a rare treat when we did. When we rode tanks we could carry the 10 in 1 on the tanks and the tank personnel often gave us some of theirs. C rations were canned rations and were available but were bulkier than K rations and the cooks usually used them to prepare meals when they could. We did have them individually when we were in a static line on the front. I recall that they had a bean and wiener or spaghetti and meatball combination that was good.

Another ration which we used only when we had to travel very lightly burdened and would be unable to be resupplied for a matter of three or four days was the D ration which was a very hard chocolate bar wrapped in a waxed cardboard box. It was very difficult to eat, hard as a rock and rather bitter but apparently three or four contained enough calories to sustain one for a day's caloric needs. It was also thought to be very constipating, probably mainly due to the fact that it provided no fiber. I usually tried to shave part of it in a canteen cup of boiling water, making a sort of chocolate drink or I would shave it into small fragments to prevent tooth fracture. We carried toilet paper in the space between the helmet liner and the straps which kept the liner from rubbing our heads.

We foraged for local foods when we could: potatoes, apples, grapes, pears etc. but eggs were the prized food when available, a welcome relief from the green powdered inedible dried eggs issued to the kitchen. We usually had one man in the section who carried a skillet and one who carried a small gasoline one burner stove that came in handy on occasion. The usual mess kit, which consisted of a round skillet like dish, a divided dish, knife, fork and spoon was designed to be carried in the knapsack which I was unable to carry with the packboard. I carried only a spoon and a canteen cup which I cooked in, drank from and ate out of . Eggs were hard to cook in it . Some of the cups had a rolled rim which retained heat long after the rest of the cup was cool so that hot drinks were cold by the time I could drink from the cup. We filed the rolled lip off in order to be able to have a hot drink. In a rare move by the bureaucracy they did come out with a revised cup without the rolled rim which permitted a soldier to drink a hot cup of coffee. When we had a chow line set up the cooks just put any food they had cooked in my cup, one layer on top of another. I would eat that and go back for the next course or for coffee. Not very elegant but it all wound up in the same place anyway.

I suppose most of us carried a talisman of some sort for "good luck." Mine was a rather battered copy of the New Testament my father had used for years. I carried it in a pipe tobacco tin in my left breast pocket and still have it as a memento. Superstition? It worked!

Rolling On

We left Angers heading for LeMans, following the 7th Armored Division, and hit very little resistance on the way. An average day of advance during much of the Northern France campaign might have been 50-60 miles, some days more, others much less. For a while the war was rather a pleasant adventure for a nineteen year old boy. We stopped in a village on a rather hot day, the kitchen truck came up and prepared a hot noonday meal for us. The cooks had loaded up on the spoils of the captured Wehrmacht liquor supply, throwing away some of the kitchen hardware, including stoves, to make way for an adequate long term supply of alcohol, something other than the vin ordinaire we encountered every day. At the head of the line the cooks were pouring Cointreau, an orange based liqueur, a full eight plus ounce canteen cup full. We quickly tossed it down to make room for the food to follow since most of us ate out of our cups, having thrown our mess kit away to save weight. I took my food, sat against the side of a barn and ate my cupful. When I finished I tried to get up and get a cup of coffee but found that I could not stand up. I didn't feel "high," just numb and immobile. The heat, fatigue and alcohol were a bit much. We were there for a bit longer, long enough for me to make my way to the truck on my own but I have had a certain respect for Cointreau ever since.

One day the column was moving on a narrow road through a forested area, trees on both sides of the road overhanging it. We were riding 2 1/2 ton trucks with the canvas tops down, one man manning a machine gun on top of the cab. Three fighter planes flew across the column at right angles to it at a very low altitude, not more than a hundred feet high. We had seen friendly fighter plane coverage all day and momentarily were unconcerned. In fact we waved to the pilots of the aircraft and one of them waved back. Then it seemed that we all realized at about the same time that those three planes had black Maltese crosses on them, instead of the white star our fighters carried, and were Me -109 fighters which looked a good bit, in silhouette, like our P-51 fighter. The column halted immediately and we poured out of the back and over the sides of the truck as rapidly as possible. I dived out on my face, Chaney hit on top of me and it seemed like fifty people were on top of me momentarily. I rolled under a log in the ditch until the planes completed their first pass, then scrambled for a place in the woods nearby. The planes came back, strafing down the column, and the sky seemed filled with white tracer bullets. They were met with a hail of small arms fire from us. One of the planes was so low he clipped branches from one of the trees, then suddenly winged over and crashed into a nearby hillside. Another was shot down with rifle and machine gun fire and the other, continuing down the column, had the misfortune to overfly an antiaircraft unit trailing us and was shot down. I contributed nothing in that encounter, I had left my carbine in the truck. I watched one of the truck drivers near me empty his rifle into the ground immediately ahead of him. He thought he was shooting at the plane and when it crashed he thought he had shot it down himself. Actually, he was more dangerous to the nearby troops than to the Germans.

For the rest of that day we dismounted every time we saw fighters overhead until we were sure they were ours.

We moved as combat teams, the Second Regimental Combat Team consisting of the Second Infantry Regiment, an artillery battalion, some combat engineers, a medical detachment, and a company or so of tanks or tank destroyers, which were somewhat lightly armored self propelled guns with 90 mm. canon on them. During the early days of the campaign many of the tanks were armed with 75 mm. cannon which would not penetrate the armor on the heavier German tanks. Later they were equiped with 76 mm. guns or 90 mm cannon, the latter were very effective.

We hit little opposition until we got to the vicinity of Chartres where the 10th Regimental Team hit moderate resistance and took a day or so to clear the town. We bypassed the town. The only view of the city that I saw was the famous cathedral spires rising from the wheat fields. We were well out of the hedgerow country; the terrain was level and ideal for mobile warfare.

It was quite hot during those August days, wearing wool OD uniforms. Several times we had no transportation and had to make long hikes in full gear: this at the time Patton's armored forces were said to be sweeping across France to victory. We would walk into a town, drop out of the column for a drink and then run to catch up. A well conditioned soldier can go far beyond his perceived ability. After exhaustion sets in you plod along mechanically, without thinking, without consciously perceiving anything. On a long march at night on level terrain we could, in effect, sleep on the march, keeping pace and interval between ourselves and the man in front, moving mechanically, halting when the column halted and moving again when it started.

We moved from the area around Chartres toward the Seine river. The night before we approached the river we had a long truck ride in a tremendous downpour. Eventually we dismounted and slept by the side of the road. Pat Halloran dug a slit trench and covered his gas mask up with the spoil from the hole. The next morning he was very upset when he couldn't find it and thought someone had stolen it. We were still carrying gas masks at the time but not long afterward we ceased to do so. I can't recall whether we were told to turn them in or just abandoned them as it became evident that poison gas was not going to be used. They were a burden and always cumbersome to carry.

We dug in on the ridge overlooking the Seine while the 10th Infantry made a heavily contested crossing at Montereau. There was heavy machine gun fire from the far bank, which was high and steep. One of the enlisted Medical Corps men got the Congressional Medal of Honor for swimming the river pulling a boatload of wounded men to safety under heavy direct machine gun fire and he did so more than once.

We were in position to see the fire fight going on but could not fire for fear of hitting friendly troops. It was just a good show for us until late in the evening when Lieutenant Myers thought he saw Germans moving toward the bridgehead. He radioed regiment that there was a German counterattack taking place. We prepared to open fire when Sergeant Pierce got a good view through his binoculars and ascertained that it was just our 2nd battalion troops taking up a new position. It was a near miss in that we did not fire on our own men nor did we call an artillery strike on them.

Two or three hours before dark we pulled back and my mortar squad and a rifle squad was sent on a motorized patrol to a little town about five miles downstream from the crossing site. We went by a back road, riding in jeeps and on light tanks, through a heavily wooded area. It was ideal country for an ambush. We passed a number of abandoned German positions as the sun was setting and arrived at the edge of the town to find that the civilians were in hiding, always an ominous sign that the enemy was thought to be near and that a fight would ensue. As we entered the town we were told that Germans had been there in strength but had crossed the river to the north bank just before we had arrived. I was not disappointed. We then went back to the company and dug in for the night.

At daylight next morning we were told we were expected to move over a hundred miles that day. C Company had the point, riding on tanks and tank destroyers, the rest of the battalion in two and a half ton trucks. We had gone about twenty miles when the column stopped. I heard an 88, the outstanding weapon of the Second World War, fire twice and we had two tanks knocked out. The Germans had elected to interfere with the planned hundred mile sojourn through beautiful central France. A Company halted about a mile west of the town of Etampes and we deployed alongside the two lane blacktop highway which luckily was ditched, the ditches providing cover from rifle and machine gun fire. There were, as usual, trees lining the road. I understand that Napoleon had required trees to be planted alongside the roads to provide shade for the peasants going to and from their fields. They also provided some concealment for American infantrymen under fire, thanks to the Little Corporal.

I might point out, for the benefit of those not familiar with the pattern, that the European farmers tend to live in small villages, perhaps a mile or so apart, and walk or ride to their fields rather than live on the actual land that they farmed. Their barns and homes in the village were usually built around a central court, usually built of stone, and could be quite formidable defense bastions if contested. The central courtyard usually contained a manure pile. They collected the urine from the livestock in sunken tanks to use for fertilizer. We occasionally flushed a German from hiding in the barn or the manure pile, the latter being the hiding place of last resort. I never found any in the urine tanks but then we never looked.

Shortly after we dismounted General Warnock pulled up in a jeep near us. He was the assistant divisional commander, in charge of divisional artillery, and that was as close as I ever saw a general officer to the front. I did learn that he spent most of his time near the front - a good brave officer. We began moving up on both sides of the road. Our artillery and 81 mm. mortars were already firing and our tanks opened up on the 88s which had knocked out the lead tanks, which were now in flames.

A common nickname for a tank was a Ronson, the brand of the most popular cigarette lighter at that time. The tanks burned brightly when hit in the engine area and the ammunition would explode, or "cook off" when they burned. It was a common sight to see tank men bailing out of the tanks with their fuel soaked clothing on fire, not a pleasant or uncommon way for them to die. We dogface infantrymen envied their ability to carry bedrolls and "luxuries" in or on the tanks and their immunity to small arms fire but not their cramped interiors and relative blindness to exterior events. The tank commanders usually left the top hatch open for visibility but when they had to "button up" under fire and close the hatch the visibility was quite limited.

We started down the road in two columns, not yet deployed on the usual broad front as skirmishers, and had moved about a hundred yards when we began receiving heavy 20 mm. fire from our right flank. I was walking in a tank track, the ground was soft from recent rain, and I hit the ground in the track at once. It was my first experience at being pinned down by automatic weapons fire and it was an unpleasant one. I looked up at the 20 mm. tracers lacing the air over us. They looked high to me. My first thought was that I was in little danger until I looked at the man in front of me and saw dirt kicking up just just behind him. It was a favorite Jerry trick, fire tracers high so that we would feel we could move freely under it and fire nontracer machine gun fire below it at waist or knee level. In that case it almost worked.

The day was grey and rainy and it was hard to locate the enemy positions in the trees and scattered buildings. Finally, the artillery began hitting on our right flank and the enemy fire slackened enough so that we could move and take cover in the roadside ditches. Our light tanks were spraying the farmhouses on our flanks with machine gun and 37 mm. light cannon fire as we moved up.

We dug in alongside the road and waited for orders. It started raining again and we waited in the rain until almost dark, then pulled out. I was crawling behind Chaney, let another man pass me and a mortar shell fragment hit him in the hand. A forward observer from the 50th Field Artillery caught a burst of 20 mm. fire in the face. It just took his face off, killing him instantly, leaving his helmet in place. John Murany had always wanted a camouflage net like the one on the observer's helmet so he just took it, helmet and all.

We pulled back and went to another road leading into town and waited until dawn to advance, to find that Jerry had pulled out during the night. On this particular occasion the French civilians were very upset over damage done to some of the buildings in the town and were insistent that the Americans repair it. It was quite different when we got in Germany; if a town was damaged there the Germans were working on it before the firing ceased. The damage did not seem very bad to my eye, at least in comparison to that we had previously seen and would later see. We hiked the rest of the day expecting further resistance but marched until dark without encountering any.

A major disappointment occurred here. We were the closest troops to Paris which was only about twenty miles away, and we had hoped to be the troops that liberated the city. Instead, the French Second Armored Division was brought up and had the privilege. Ernest Hemingway went through 5th Division lines to enter Paris; there was really nothing in the way of resistance in front of us.

The 2nd Infantry went into divisional reserve. We got a two day break and headed for Nogent-sur-Seine, took the city and crossed the river with little resistance. We headed toward Regent-sur-Seine drawing sniper fire as we marched. That night we hiked all night through a dense forest, carrying all our heavy equipment. It was a clear moonlight night, the moonlight filtering through the trees was quite pretty but I had little appreciation for it. There was a dense undergrowth of thorny ground cover and I thought my packboard that night would break my neck. I have understood that we were in the forest of Fontainebleau that night but we never saw the famous chateau. It was not included on our tour. We spent most of our time in the low rent districts.

We stopped just before daylight to get some sleep in an open field. I started looking for some hay to sleep on, saw what I thought was a sheaf of hay and found that it was wired together. I also found out the hard way that it was a beehive. That was the last time I picked things up without examining them.

Cowboy and Indian Fighting in Champagne Country

Thou shalt not be afraid of the terror by night;
Nor for the arrow that flieth by day;
A thousand may fall at thy side,
Ten thousand at thy right hand;
But it shall not come nigh thee.

91st Psalm

From Regent sur Seine we went north through Suzzane to the Marne at Epernay. The evening before we reached the Marne we were riding on C Company, 818thTank Destroyers and stopped at a crossroad to get directions. We had run off of our maps and the supply people were unable to keep up with our advance. Maps frequently had to be dropped by air. In all, eight tons of maps were dropped to the Third Army in the advance across France.

There were a few scattered buildings, typical one or two story stone French village buildings. Chaney and I got a drink of water from the villagers and sat down by one of the tank destroyers when a FW (Focke Wulfe) 190 came out of nowhere at an altitude of about 30 feet at right angles to the column. We figured that he was just looking us over preparing for a strafing run so we ducked around behind one of the buildings to a cellar entrance behind the building. Two men in blue denim farmer-type clothes and black berets came down into the cellar entrance with us. Very shortly thereafter three P-47 American fighters came over at low altitude, apparently in pursuit of the FW-190. I presume Jerry got away as he was at low altitude flying toward the north and a minute or so ahead of the P- 47s. The two civilians came out of the cellar entrance with us and one of them commented "Those Focke Wulfes are bastards, aren't they?". I asked where he had learned to speak such unaccented English and he told us that they were B-17 bomber gunners who had been shot down near Sedan and were making their way back to American lines in the French underground. The lines were fluid at the time and they had experienced little difficulty once the French picked them up and provided clothing.

We learned that we were to make a crossing of the Marne River that night, the 28th of August. The Germans were expected to contest it, making a stand on the north bank. They had blown the bridge, some of the FFI had attempted to construct a foot bridge but had been killed in the attempt. We rode to within a mile or two of Maruial, about 5 miles east of Epernay, dismounted, and marched to the river. The center span of the bridge had been blown; we put rubber pontoons in the blown area, laid planks on them forming a foot bridge and walked across without opposition. A short distance further on we came upon a canal but were able to cross it by moving upstream to a lock and walking across the closed lock gates. The lack of resistance was a surprise.

The company dug in on a rather high chalky hill in a large vineyard in the heart of the Champagne district. The grapes were ripe; they may not have been the table type of grape, but we stuffed ourselves with them, after digging in the mortars and zeroing in on a draw in the terrain which would have been an ideal approach by Jerry, should he attack us. Sergeant Cody, who spoke French reasonably well and acted as company interpreter, went down into Epernay and brought back some wine and bread. It rained a good bit but we were comfortable and took life easy until the engineers got a bridge which could support armored traffic across the Marne. We remounted our tank destroyers and headed for Reims.

It was overcast and intermittently rainy as we approached Reims. We passed through a number of small villages and the people gave us an enthusiastic welcome. One soldier was injured when a bottle of champagne thrown by the "welcoming committee" struck him in the head. A case of champagne thrown onto the tank destroyer I rode knocked the antenna off of the tank destroyer and, in effect, disabled it to a degree. Perhaps the first armored vehicle knocked out by champagne! The TDs were loaded down with the stuff. One of the mortar squad sergeants proceeded to try to keep consumption up with reception and was rendered ineffective for a day or two.

We moved down a long gradual slope toward Reims which was in clear view but, as we descended the hill approaching the town, we received heavy small arms fire from our right flank. We attacked the enemy in that direction, moving over some hills which had been fought over in the First World War. Old trenches and shell holes were overgrown with grass and brush but rusty barbed wire entanglements were still there. We captured six or eight Germans moving along some paths in the brush, attempting to escape.

Some platoons from C Company crossed a canal and our armor could not follow. When the infantry had moved away from the canal they were attacked by German tanks. It was dark and Jerry turned spotlights on the C Company men, killing or wounding several. They had to withdraw back across the canal.

As daylight broke we moved into town, taking some sniper fire. We cleared the town without a great deal of opposition. As was the case in most towns not heavily fought over, we were welcomed ecstatically. To our surprise there were quite a few American airmen in the town, usually dressed in the French peasant uniform of denims and a beret. They had been shot down in the Sedan area and had made their way via the underground to Reims. They jokingly said that they were sorry to see us since they were living with French girls and now would have to return to flying combat missions. In the area in front of the city hall the civilians were dragging collaborators in for a great mob scene. Men who had aided the Germans were summarily shot, the clothing was ripped off the women and their heads were shaved. In a situation like that I wondered how much of the violence was justified and how much might just be based on personal animosities. Certainly some of those people probably deserved their fate, from the response of the mob, but some of it may have been a part of the friction between the followers of DeGaulle and the communist underground.

We spent the night in Reims and then started for Verdun. The second day of that advance, a clear warm day, the First Battalion was in a motorized column on the left, the Second Battalion on our right. Dust rising from a road on our right was visible for a good portion of the day as we moved through somewhat hilly and wooded country. We assumed that the dust was from Second Battalion movement. Our fighter bombers were overhead a good bit of the day; our vehicles carried vivid orange identification markers on them while the Germans carried a bright red square with a swastika, if they showed any identification. Most of them did not as we had air superiority. Some of our planes flew rather low so we thought they would pick up enemy columns with ease. The two separate roads converged gradually as we advanced.

About three hours before dark we hit a roadblock, twenty Krauts or so with two machine guns. The TDs we were riding on opened up with machine gun fire and 76 mm. cannon fire. The Germans began running or giving up. One German running across a field caught a direct hit from a 76 mm. shell. One second there was a running man, the next an explosion, a puff of smoke and then nothing. We let six or seven of them come in and surrender and then moved on. Shortly thereafter we spotted a German tank, a TD got in a couple of hits on it but it got away. We started up a wooded hill when one of the light artillery spotting planes, a Piper Cub type, dropped down and signalled that enemy armor was up ahead. Almost immediately after that the lead truck received a direct hit from an 88, killing three men and wounding three or four. I didn't know most of the men in that platoon but did know Cholipenichuk who was killed and Montain who was wounded.

Battalion headquarters must have figured we were running into a "snow-storm", a term used to imply lots of small arms tracer fire. They halted us and did some reorganization. We dismounted and resumed the advance, the first and second platoons on the left of the road, the third and weapons platoon on the right. It was hilly terrain, second growth hardwood in full green foliage and full of old trenches and shell holes, a part of the Argonne Forest so heavily fought over in World War One. The road we were on converged with another near the top of the hill, visibility through the foliage was limited to only a few feet until we found a narrow path near the top of the hill, where we were almost to the road on top of the hill.

Lieutenants Meyers and Russell, the latter the third platoon commander, slipped across the road on reconnaissance. Shortly after they did so a German tank came down the road from our right to the trail we were on and turned up into it. A half track full of infantry and a motorcycle followed it. We could not see them through the leaves though they were not over thirty feet away. When they began talking we knew it was not the Second Battalion which we expected to be there. Other half tracks loaded with infantry pulled up on the roadway above us. We had no bazookas (the American shoulder fired antitank weapon) or antitank grenades so we had to withdraw, the Krauts close behind us.

Lt. Meyers and Lt. Russell were cut off on the other side of the road. Meyers was captured but Russell waited until after dark to slip back across the road and escaped. On one previous occasion Meyers asked a soldier to tell a captured wounded German paratrooper "Tell him I'm a Jew." I have often wondered what happened to Lt. Meyers but have never heard from him again. We dropped down to a small clearing in the forest and waited a few minutes until dark. The moon came out and with it a German patrol but they only probed to a point near us but made no immediate contact. We then slipped down to the bottom of the hill and into our own lines.

The first and second platoons on the left of the road were caught and pinned down by machine gun and small arms fire most of the night. Captain Trimble, Cannon Company's commander, who was with the two rifle platoons, directed artillery fire on a German tank while he was under the tank and knocked it out. He certainly had a good vantage point from which to direct fire. It was a little like the episode in which Audie Murphy mounted a knocked out American tank and manned its machine gun during a counter attack when the Germans overran his platoon. He used the radio to call down artillery fire on his position and was asked how close the enemy was to him. He replied "Hold the phone, I'll let you speak to one of the sons of bitches."

This was a rather typical episode in the fluid war across northern France. The Germans were surprised by the speed of our movement, frequently lost contact with units on their flanks and, because of our air superiority, often had no idea that we had units between them and the German border. They did set up road blocks but encounters between large units were usually accidental, short and violent.

At daylight the next day the Germans had pulled out and we learned that we had run into the rear guard of the 29th Panzer Division which we had often made contact with all across France. They were trying to get across the Meuse at Verdun but the 10th Infantry had already occupied the city and the Germans had to swing to the north to get out of the trap.

We outposted in the area for two days, then went into Verdun on the east bank of the Meuse and sat with the rest of the 5th Infantry Division and the 7th Armored Division, out of gas, out of ammunition and largely out of food. There were only two thousand gallons of gas in the entire division. One thousand gallons/day were needed for cooking. There was little to cook. We had captured a German warehouse, stocked largely with Limburger cheese, ersatz coffee and black bread and that is all we had to eat for several days. We also drew some German rabbit fur jackets from a captured warehouse in Verdun though we were a bit reluctant to wear them as it was felt that Jerry would react harshly if we were captured wearing German uniform materials.

The area around Verdun was still a wasteland of devastated land from the last war, Over a million casualties had been sustained in the area one could see with the naked eye from the top of Fort Douamont on a hill above Verdun. The Ossuary at Verdun contained the bones of over forty thousand men, loosely lying in the lower floor of the building. Seventeen thousand closely aligned grave markers, the cross arms touching, lie facing the east in front of the Ossuary. There is nothing else in the world like it, thank goodness.

This fuel situation was a result of the attempt to sustain two major drives into Germany, one to the north under Montgomery and one under Patton directly across northern France toward the Rhineland. Historians still argue whether diversion of most of the supplies to one or the other could have resulted in a rapid end to the war. At the time the Third Army front extended from Brest, in Brittany, to Verdun and from the Loire to near the Luxembourg border. The "Red Ball Express" was developed to shuttle truck loads of supplies from the ports in Normandy to the front, driving nonstop day and night, but our movement was too rapid for them to keep up. Part of the problem was also due to the fact that General J. C. "Jesus Christ" Lee, commander of the ComZ or Communications Zone, used 25,000 gallons of fuel in moving his headquarters to Paris in spite of Eisenhower's orders not to do so.

We stayed in the Verdun area from the first to the sixth of September, down to one clip of rifle ammunition per man in some units and eating what little we could scrounge locally. A task force of the Sixth Cavalry Group had entered the outskirts of Metz with no opposition but the Germans had moved into Metz in strength and kicked them out, mining the approach roads and occupying permanent fortifications, some of them dating back to 1870 and beyond. The cowboy and Indian wars were over but we were not yet aware of it. The campaign in Northern France was, relative to what was to follow, one of wine and roses: good weather, rapid movement, low casualties and a population that welcomed their liberation.The big drums were in position and, for me, the real war was about to begin.

Letter, August 27th-I'm fine and dandy, about as satisfied as I can be over here so don't worry about me. I'm getting along OK even if I can't speak French.

August 30th-I'm beginning to like France a little more than I did. Even though I can't speak the language it's certainly not hard to understand that the people are glad to see us.

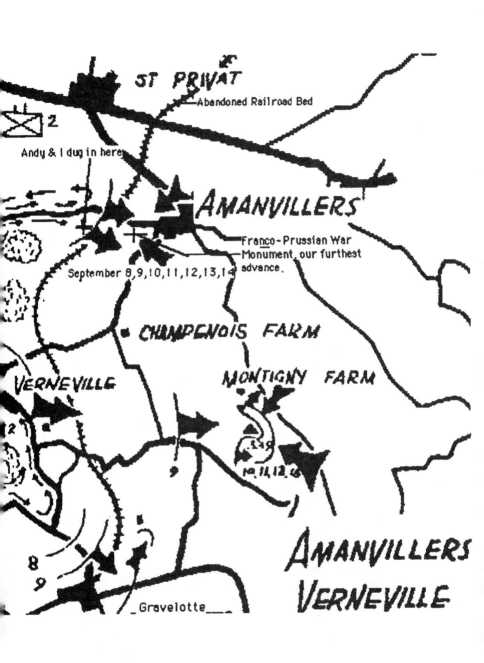

ST PRIVAT

—Abandoned Railroad Bed

2

Andy & I dug in here

AMANVILLERS

Franco-Prussian War
Monument, our furthest
advance.

September 8,9,10,11,12,13,14

CHAMPENOIS FARM

MONTIGNY FARM

VERNEVILLE

2

9

10, 11, 12, 13

8
9

Gravelotte

AMANVILLERS
VERNEVILLE

Metz, The Battle That Should Not Have Been

Amanvillers

I hate that drum's discordant sound,
Parading round, and round, and round:
To thoughtless youth it pleasure yields,
And lures from cities and from fields,
To sell their liberty for charms
Of tawdry lace, and glittering arms;
And when Ambition's voice commands,
To march, and fight, and fall, in foreign lands.
                    The Drum-*John Scott of Amway*

This coming battle really was a complete break in the usual Third Army tactic of bypassing and surrounding enemy strong points but it developed, in part, because we simply stumbled into it without knowledge of the true situation. Metz had been an object of military significance for centuries.The Romans had used it as a major fortified area and it had only been taken by storm, though repeatedly fought over, by Attila the Hun in A.D. 451.

The city is largely situated on islands in the Moselle River and is surrounded by hills. Vauban, a French engineer, constructed forts at the bridgeheads into the city in the eighteenth century and one of them, Fort Bellecroix, was an important stronghold in the fighting we were to face. In 1867, just before the Franco-Prussian war, four detached forts were started by the French on the high ground two to three miles from the city. They were not completed by the beginning of the Franco-Prussian war but the Germans, who took Alsace-Lorraine from the French after defeating them, finished the forts and constructed a complete line of fortifications before the First World War. They completed a ring of nine small forts surrounding the city and in the 1890s they developed massive fortifications on the high ground on the west bank of the Moselle, constructed of concrete with multiple underground floors as barracks, interconnected tunnels from one to the other, 100 and 150 mm. armored rotating gun turrets, concrete pillboxes and armored observation posts. All these were heavily camouflaged and mutually supporting so that the guns of one fort could fire on the other forts if an enemy succeeded in blowing up the ten- foot- high steel fences and barbed wire surrounding the forts, crossing the moats which were twenty feet deep and scaling the walls of the moat to gain access to the top of the fort. These had their own electrical systems, water supply and other basic communications systems. The forts started in 1899(Forts Lorraine, de Guise, Jeanne d'Arc, and Driant) were huge, Fort Driant covered 355 acres. The major forts were surrounded by a moat sixty feet wide and twenty feet deep with numerous firing ports covering the moat from both the inner and outer walls of the moat. Fort Driant in particular was regarded as the key to Metz. It's guns dominated the banks of the Moselle. Metz was the most heavily fortified city in the world.

The attack on Metz by the Third Army will probably be the last time in history that a direct assault will have been made on a city permanently fortified to such a degree. Metz itself, the center of a highway system, was the key to the Saar valley and entry into the Rhineland of Germany. It was in a gap between the mountainous terrain of the Ardennes and the Vosges Mountains. The amazing thing is that we attacked these fortifications completely unaware that they were there and it was several weeks before we were able to obtain plans of the forts from French engineer officers who had been stationed in the forts. In many cases we not only did not know the plan of the forts; we were totally unaware that they even existed until we drew fire from them.

The area on the west bank of the Moselle that we were entering was defended by students of the German OCS (Officers Candidate School) in Metz. We were later informed that the requirements for entry into the school were a year of combat experience, proven ability as leaders in combat, age under 28 years, perfect physical condition and fanatical Nazism. They were, beyond reasonable doubt, the best enemy troops we faced during the war, better than any SS or Panzer troops. In addition there were 1500 members of a noncommisioned officers school in the area, all experienced men. These troops all fought in the role of ordinary soldiers. In the area around Gravelotte, St. Privat, Verneville and Amanvillers there was, in 1870, a famous battle between the French and Germans. The French were attempting to break out of Metz to the west but were repulsed, fell back into the city and sat there until the wars end. Fighting here became somewhat the equivalent of attacking American OCS students, all with extensive combat experience, defending a heavily fortified Gettysburg where they had conducted repeated military exercises and were intimately familiar with the terrain. They knew the most likely places we would set up mortars, artillery pieces etc. before we even arrived on the scene.

The German defense here was quite different from their usual method of defense which often consisted of holding a position with a rather small force and reserving a major force for a violent counterattack when the attacking enemy was disorganized. In the Metz area they had reinforced concrete pill boxes and forts and defended them with the maximum available force.

We started hiking east again but had to stop just outside of Conflans, about eighteen miles west of Metz. The third platoon outposted Conflans, the rest of the company dug in on the outskirts just west of town, halted again by lack of supplies. We stayed there one night. The next morning Lt. King told us "Well, men, we're going to take Metz today," and we loaded up on 50th Field Artillery trucks, picked up the third platoon en route and headed to Metz.

We had gone about ten miles when the column halted; we dismounted and started hiking. Our artillery began setting up and we knew that B Company, who had the point, had run into opposition. I could hear shells hitting up front as rifle and machine gun fire began to open up. We moved up to a railroad bank and crossed an open field into a dense forest, receiving sniper and artillery fire as we crossed the tracks. As we moved into the forest sniper fire increased, the sound of the bullets that were very close snapping or popping as they passed near by, in contrast to the somewhat duller crack of the sound from the rifle, heard from some distance. At a distance in front of us we could, from time to time, see a church tower which was obviously being used as an observation point calling down accurate fire on us, a source of trouble until we left the area. We swung to the left and followed the railroad toward the east, crossing an open field and drawing intense small arms fire as we did so. A section runner hit the dirt and stayed there all day, then went back to battalion headquarters and we never saw him again. He really was older than most of us and in rather poor condition to be an infantryman. The rest of the company crossed back over the railroad embankment which gave us shelter from the small arms fire from the east of us, returned the fire and stayed there until an hour or so before dark. B and C Companies were engaged in an intense fire fight to our left but we had no idea where any other friendly troops were. There was a small village to our rear, whether friendly or enemy troops were in it we did not know, which caused considerable uneasiness. As it turned out, no troops were in it. Andy and I dug in, setting up the mortar, preparing for any eventuality.

As soon as daylight began to fade we formed up and prepared to attack Amanvillers, the town to our front, which was the source of the fire we were receiving. We moved along the edge of the woods onto the old abandoned railroad; the center of the roadbed was sunken to such a degree that it was almost like a trench and afforded some cover from small arms fire. Just after dark we began to move out but Jerry apparently knew what we were doing and began laying a lot of mortar and air burst artillery fire on us, causing a considerable number of casualties. Cassidy, one of the men from my home county, was wounded there and never came back up to the company again. For some reason the attack was called off; we pulled back to the first rail embankment and stayed until the next afternoon. During the night one platoon of C Company and a heavy machine gun section of D Company were surrounded and captured.

I might add here a comment about the different types of artillery fire we received. There were two major types of artillery pieces: howitzers which fired at a moderately high trajectory so that the descending shell could be heard coming in with a rumbling or rushing sound, and high velocity rifles, like the 88 mm. gun the Germans used so well which could be used as an antiaircraft, an antipersonnel or an antitank weapon. The howitzers used against us fired 100 mm. or 150 mm. shells, usually exploding on contact with the ground but the time of explosion could be timed so that the shell burst in the air, preferably at a height of only a few feet. The shell striking the ground threw shrapnel out in an inverted cone pattern and if one were lying on the ground the chances of being hit were reduced. The air burst threw shrapnel in a round ball like pattern and one could be hit, even in a foxhole. Tree bursts, wherein the shell struck overhead limbs and exploded, were as effective as air bursts. These shells had an effective range on explosion of 25 to 35 yards but could kill even at a range of 50-75 yards if a fragment hit just right.

Mortar shells were lobbed in a very high trajectory; they were designed to drop in on the back of hills or into gun emplacements which had been dug into the ground. They could be heard only as a low pitched whisper just before they hit. I could hear them coming in better than most people which was useful since mortars were a prime target for other mortars. The shell exploded on contact and had a cone shaped effective pattern of 20-30 yards. The 88 mm. rifle had a muzzle velocity of about 3000 feet per second and was only heard as a sound like silk tearing violently a millisecond or so before it hit so that there was no time to take cover. The shrapnel was thrown primarily in the direction of the gunfire, with little being blown to the rear.

Mortar and artillery fire were particularly effective against mortar and machine gun detachments since the rifle platoons preceded the heavy weapons. If a company was on the move the artillery fire tended to strike the trailing platoons once they were zeroed in on the line of advance, which usually took some time to do. The rifle platoons were more vulnerable to rifle and machine gun fire which usually opened up before the artillery once the enemy was sighted at close quarters. However, if the rifle platoons were pinned down by small arms fire the artillery and mortars would zero in on them with devastating effect. Most of the casualties in the mortar section were from shrapnel, usually when we were caught in the open without a chance to dig in. Usually in an attack we would dig in, set up the mortars and begin firing on possible enemy positions before the rifle platoons advanced, leapfrogging forward as they occupied ground. The range of the 60 mm. mortar was roughly 2000 yards; it was fairly accurate if there was no wind but the high trajectory and low velocity rendered accuracy vulnerable to wind, which we tried to allow for.

The next morning the mortar section dug in behind a railroad bank and we began firing at extreme range, trying to keep an observer out of the church tower in Amanvillers. One of the 818th TDs pulled up near us and began firing at the tower. We pulled out and jumped off with the company, attacking the town. Our initial firing position had been behind the railroad bank to the west of the old abandoned roadbed. Before we jumped off Jerry began throwing heavy artillery fire into the field between the two parallel rail road beds,. About 75 yards separated the two but it seemed to be an interminable distance as events developed. The roadbeds were built up about eight or nine feet high. As the artillery fire came in we could hear it striking the next field and the shrapnel singing overhead. Hank Terzago, the platoon runner, ran up on the bank, called out, "There's lots of artillery over here. The hell with the artillery, let's go!" And over we went after him. As I crossed the railroad I got the shock of my life. The field was black with bursting artillery shells and the field was cluttered with dead and wounded men. We also received small arms fire from our left but it was not as lethal as the shelling.

There was a ditch in the field, running from one embankment to the other. It was only inches deep but gave a little cover and seemed like Paradise compared to the rest of the field. It was filled with dead and wounded; we had to dodge around them as we crossed the field. We finally got to the relative shelter of the far bank and began to dig in as rapidly as possible. I was an ammo bearer and had to go back across the field time after time to the company ammunition dump as we began expending our mortar shells in support of the rifle platoons. We fired over a thousand mortar shells that day. Since we could only carry eighteen rounds at a time we made many trips back and forth. Luckily, after the first few minutes Jerry shifted some of the fire closer to his lines as the attack by the rifle platoons developed and, though shell fire was still heavy in the area between the guns and the ammo dump, it slackened there to some degree. On one trip a piece of shrapnel about four inches long struck my helmet, piercing the outer steel shell, lodging in the helmet but not piercing the inner helmet liner. You might say it rang my bell. The helmet undoubtedly saved my life.

The first and second platoons were the assault platoons, the third was in reserve. Initially the rifle platoons made good progress in the face of intense small arms and artillery fire until they reached barbed wire obstacles. These were in the form of four or five foot coils of barbed wire and strung wire aprons three or four feet high and five or six feet wide. Lt. King went forward to evaluate the situation and found that there were covered foxholes manned by Germans behind our forward lines, between the forward platoons and the third platoon. He had to commit the third platoon to clearing the foxholes, losing its firepower assisting the assault platoons. The third platoon became pinned down along with the rest of the company and remained so until dark.

That night Lt. King wanted to pull the entire mortar section out into the field with the rifle platoons. Sgt. Pierce argued with him with the final result that only the first squad was sent into the field in front of us. A prime military axiom is that mortars should take advantage of their range. That simply means that, since they have a range of about two thousand yards, they can usually find a somewhat sheltered position to fire from and thereby reduce their casualties as well as be more effective if their fire is disturbed as little as possible. As a rule, the gunner and assistant gunner fired from a sitting position and were more vulnerable to enemy fire than a prone rifleman if they were in a similar exposed position. The next morning the company was pinned down again, The fire was so heavy the first mortar squad was unable to fire. Sgt. Cody, the squad leader, was wounded when a bullet hit a clip in his rifle belt, exploding the shells in it and causing extensive wounds in his hip and kidneys. The rest of the squad was able to get out but lost their mortar and ammunition. That night I went out with Lt. Murphy to reconnoiter and passed some mortar ammunition on the way out. Later Chaney and I went out to get it, walked by it in the dark and went a good hundred and fifty yards beyond our outposts. We realized finally that we had passed B Company's truck that had been knocked out the first day of the battle and could see the details of the town all too clearly, dangerously so. We did not linger but picked up the mortar shells on the way back to our lines.

It is said that the Second World War was the last chivalric war. The Americans, British, French and Germans observed the Geneva Convention in terms of the conduct of war to a considerable degree. The Japanese and Russians did not. At Amanvillers the elite German infantry actually helped pick up our wounded at night and carried them to an exchange point, turning them over to our medics. Also, they did not fire on our medics who wore distinctive white arm bands and helmets with a Red Cross on them. We reciprocated.

Before daylight the next morning the company pulled back to the abandoned road bed where the mortars were dug in. We sat there for three days watching an intense artillery bombardment of enemy lines and P-47s of the Ninth Air Force strafe and dive bomb continually. It was a striking show; they were hitting about three to five hundred yards in front of us and it seemed that nothing could live there. The planes came in just over our heads, made a run and repeated it until they were out of ammunition. Two of them were shot down;

one fell behind enemy lines, another made it back over our lines and the pilot bailed out safely. As events later showed, it was all fruitless. We should have known it was, during the aerial attack we received some of the heaviest artillery fire of the battle. The enemy was, in large part, safe in deep permanent fortifications or in an underground section of a quarry. The bombardment had little effect, though it was quite spectacular.

Then orders came down for another attack. We had a terrific preliminary barrage and it seemed as though things might go well for us. Colonel Rolfe, the regimental commander, and General Sylvester, the 7th Armored's commanding general, were both there watching it. The regiment was acting as a detached force under 7th Armored command.

I remember giving the OK sign with circled thumb and forefinger to my friend Vaughn in one of the machine gun squads as he moved out in the attack. He was a colorful fellow, slender, quite handsome, blond mustache, wearing some German parachute silk as a bandanna; an orphan who had been brought up by a family in a circus. A few minutes later he was dead. The attack went well, the advance went almost to the edge of the town. The barrage had disrupted the barbed wire. However the company was pinned down again. The 7th Armored sent in a company of tanks, sixteen in all, to try to assist in the attack but all but one of them were knocked out in less than half an hour by dug in 88 mm. guns and Tiger tanks. The field was littered with burning tanks, their ammunition exploding and the tank personnel bailing out, some on fire. Bad way to die. Some of the riflemen got as far as a monument to a German unit that had fought on that very field in the Franco-Prussian War but that is as close as they ever got to the town.

The commanding general of the 7th Armored Division ordered us to make another attack but Colonel Blakefield, our battalion commander, refused. We could not take Amanvillers with one thousand men in the battalion. It seemed unlikely we could do so with the remnant of two hundred or so. A Company was down to fewer than thirty men from an initial strength of over two hundred.

We were relieved by the 351st Infantry Regiment of the 90th Division who attacked in regimental strength the objective we attacked in battalion strength. They failed and the town was never taken by storm. It was bypassed on the final assault on Metz and held out until the Germans there were almost surrounded and the remaining troops surrendered. It was only five miles from Metz but it took two more bloody months of fighting before we entered Metz. The dead lay there until the battle was ended.

The men of the German OCS Regiment were evacuated just before the encirclement, their leadership qualities were too valuable to be lost after it became apparent that the city must fall. They were awarded a special arm band

-"Metz,1944"- as a mark of distinction.

The Third Battalion of the 2nd Infantry attacked Gravelotte and the Second Battalion struck at Verneville while we were attacking Amanvillers, all unsuccessfully and with heavy casualties. While the 2nd Infantry was thus engaged the 10th and 11th Infantry were making a successful crossing of the Moselle in the face of bitter resistance. Almost the entire Second Battalion of the 11th Infantry was wiped out in their crossing. We did, by maintaining pressure on the fortifications on the west bank, prevent the elite OCS unit there from reinforcing the German troops at the river crossing.

During the month of September the 5th Infantry Division had 5180 casualties, largely in the rifle companies, in effect temporarily destroying its ability to function as an infantry unit. Most of the casualties were in a five day period. From the division's entry into Normandy until the end of the war the division had a total of 25,000 casualties, roughly half of which were "nonbattle" from battle fatigue, broken bones, infectious disease etc., . That is more casualties than the United States suffered in the Revolutionary War, the War of 1812 and the Mexican War combined. September was the division's bloodiest month though A Company suffered as badly, and the weapons platoon worse, in November.

Infantry troops made up about ten percent of all the troops in the Army and took seventy percent of the casualties.

Letter, September 6-I'm getting along fine and can't complain. The weather is getting a little cool but we can take that along with the rest. The bees over here are worse than flies are at home,hardly a day goes by without my getting three or four stings.

In the nineteen eighties I went back to Amanvillers, now a quite peaceful village and walked across the field to the monument. I remember we fired our mortars at a machine gun dug in near it. The marble on the monument is pocked with bullet and shrapnel marks but the inscriptions are still legible. I found the remains of a foxhole, burrowed into the bank of the railroad, that Andy Carpenter and I had dug. We slept in it then, cramped and uncomfortable, and took shelter in it from enemy fire. It was somewhat balloon shaped with no room to stretch out but it saved our lives from several near misses. There was a two story building a couple of hundred yards from our foxhole and the current residents still clearly recall those violent days. The two rail beds are still there, both abandoned now. The church steeple, which we never managed to knock down and which looked down on us like an evil source of enemy intelligence, still dominates the skyline of the village. Aside from the old collapsing foxholes behind the rail bed there is no trace of the violence that took place there. Oddly enough the area around Amanvillers, Gravelotte and St. Privat is dotted with monuments to German and French units that fought there in 1870. There is a museum detailing events of that battle but there is not a single marker commemorating the battle in 1944.

The Moselle

We moved back some distance from Amanvillers and took up positions in a wooded area just outside a small town. There we stayed for three days, drawing replacements for the casualties and replacing equipment lost in battle. The American army usually kept units that had sustained heavy casualties, replacing the men with troops arriving from America or, occasionally, as they did late in the fall campaign which had high casualty rates, stripping some of the rear echelon units of men to serve as "cannon fodder." The German army tended to disband decimated units, take the few remaining men from several units and putting them all together in task forces, usually named after the unit commander. I believe the American method was better as there was some continuity of officers and noncommissioned officers as well as some esprit de corps.

Following the replenishment of men and material we were driven south to join the rest of the division on the east bank of the Moselle. That evening, the 15th of September, we rode until we came to a bridge which had been blown up and had collapsed, obstructing the road. Dismounting, we hiked through a small village destroyed by artillery fire, down a small valley through Pagny and then down along the river to a bridgehead over the river near Arnaville as darkness fell. There were quite a few troops and vehicles in Arnaville. I recall that there was an unusual deep silence as we passed through the ruined town, broken only by the mutter of artillery fire and occasional small arms fire in the distance. We passed through town to a railroad underpass and halted for a short period while Jerry opened up with some artillery fire which fell quite near us but the underpass provided fairly good cover for the men in it. From there we moved down a rather high bank and onto the river bottom.

The east bank of the Moselle valley is a rather high one, rough, hilly, and covered to a large degree by forest. As we moved onto the river bottom we could see the flash of German artillery pieces as they fired toward us from the high ground and we could both see and hear the flash and thump of enemy mortars as they fired on our troop position. It was well after dark but there was bright moonlight with clouds scudding across the face of the moon. The pontoon bridge area across the river was plainly visible to Jerry from the high ground to the north of us in the area of Fort Driant. As a result, Chemical Warfare smoke units were deployed to obscure their view of the bridge. The moonlight, the variable cloudiness, the smoke we moved through and the relative silence with only the sound of our foottsteps to be heard, gave a very eerie, dreamlike quality to the scene. We moved in two single files along the approach, one on each side of the road, with about a ten yard interval between men to minimize casualties from a single shell. Artillery fire was coming in very close and we had a number of casualties as we approached the bridge. I stepped across a body lying beside the road, thinking it was a dead German initially but a second glance proved it to be Lt. King, our company commander. He was a fine soldier and a compassionate officer, one of the best.

As we approached the bridge a column of Sherman medium tanks came up through the company and, just as we got to the bridge, they pulled up alongside the weapons platoon. The columns of both men and armor had halted. The noise of the tanks brought on heavy shelling, most of it in our immediate area. The Combat Engineers, who did the bridging, took a lot of casualties that night trying to keep the bridge operational. Moving off the bridge, we followed a tree lined dirt road to the foot of the hills on the east side of the river under constant accurate artillery fire. Luckily there was a ditch alongside the road which gave a good bit of shelter.

We moved up the hill to the east, passing through several badly shelled villages into a bivouac area along with some 7th Armored Division tanks in a dense pine forest. The following morning we took up holding position in a pine forest to the south of Arry, passing a number of dead American and German soldiers as we moved into the remnant of the old Hindenburg line, dating back to World War One, which ran along the crest of the hill we were on. I still dream of moving, on a gray rainy day, through a pine forest up a hill with scattered dead German soldiers in their field gray uniforms, faces gray in death, lying about on the red clay ground; the only such dreams of war I have had in recent years. No violent action, just dead Germans and silence. We moved into the old overgrown trenches which overlooked a small village and a number of our own artillery units, the latter dug in around the village.

The weather, typical for Lorraine in the fall, was miserable with steady drizzling rain from which there was no escape. We sat in the woods and attempted to heat coffee to combat the misery of the weather. A new company commander, a Captain Scully , joined us there. He was a big rough looking man and when Chaney and I first talked to him we thought he was an enlisted replacement as we could see no insignia on him. Most officers wore no collar insignia but wore a vertical white band on the back of their helmet for identification; some did wear green badges of insignia rather than the dress gold or silver insignia. Company commanders were prime targets for snipers.

From this position we moved, in the evening over roads deep in mud, down into the valley in heavy rain and under heavy shelling. The enemy artillery fire was very accurate, localized to the road to an uncanny degree. We had a number of casualties as a result, one of whom was a mortar section replacement, Sgt. Light, who had just joined us and was, as was often the case, wounded before he could ever fire a shot at the enemy. We finally dug in on the edge of a forest and had hot food for two days. On the evening of September 19th we got the order to attack the village of Coin-sur-Sielle. Our last hot meal for several weeks was served and we drew field rations for several days.

Coin-sur-Sielle and Loiville

Yea, though I walk through the valley of the shadow of death
I shall fear no evil for thou art with me.
23rd Psalm

On the morning of the 20th of September we moved out to attack the villages of Loiville and Coin-sur-Sielle. We moved up a little trail through a forest, passed through K Company's position and out into the open. As we moved into the open and up a hill we came under direct observation and immediately received artillery fire. Captain Scully called "Fix bayonets. Charge, you sons of bitches" and was almost instantly wounded. I don't know the extent of his injury but he had about as short a combat career as any company commander we had. As we moved along a small stream running in a deep ravine a lot of outgoing "mail" (our own artillery shells) passed over us. Two of the new replacements, Stamps and Stamper, had never had artillery fire pass so low overhead and dived six or eight feet into the creek bed, packboards and all. It was a wonder they weren't injured by the packboards as they fell. Enemy artillery fire increased as we moved up a hill and we began to receive small arms fire from our right flank. We dug in and began to fire, the rifle platoons pressed the attack;Trigger acting as platoon sergeant and directing mortar fire. About 30 minutes after we opened fire enemy artillery fire zeroed in on us but we had dug in well and no one was hit.

The 7th Armored Division began an attack on our right but was unable to make headway. As a result we were subjected to incessant small arms fire from that flank. We beat off several counterattacks and, as it began to grow dark, we moved up to a pillbox on the outskirts of Loiville. We could see flashes from enemy artillery to the southeast. Occasionally they fired nebelwerfers, which we called "screaming meemies," at us. They were large rockets which made a tremendous noise as they were fired. and packed a tremendous wallop on impact but were rather inaccurate. They were also visible as they begin their outgoing flight, trailing a long stream of sparks. The visual and auditory effect was terrifying and magnified by the fact that they were fired, often eight to ten in a sequential manner, with only a second or two between them.

We moved, again, to a point on the outskirts of Coin-sur-Seille near a walled cemetery and dug in in a very muddy potato field. Early the next morning we began receiving artillery and mortar fire from the east bank of the Seille river which lay about 200 yards to our front. Our position was readily visible to Jerry from an old chateau across the river. Whenever we moved or fired our mortars we received immediate counter battery fire. O'Connor and I had dug a fairly deep foxhole. Several artillery shells fell within three or four feet of our foxhole, literally covering us up with dirt. O'Connor, the gunner in my squad, who had received a Silver Star for heroism in Normandy, curled up in the hole and commented "Nickell, they're going to kill us all."

Andy Carpenter and I, tired of lying in the mud, decided to go into the hamlet of Loiville and get some hay or straw for the bottom of our foxholes so we walked into the village in broad daylight and returned with some straw. As might be expected, we received some mortar and artillery fire on our position within minutes of our return. Moving in broad daylight in full view of the enemy was sheer folly, pinpointing our position. Trigger reinforced the point by making us dig a large hole for the CP (company command post.).

I am glad to say that we were not the only ones to make such a stupid mistake. The German aid men wore a long white capes with a red cross on both front and back as well as white helmets with a red cross on them. One day they came along the German lines carrying a stretcher as if they were picking up a casualty, stopping now and then next to a well camouflaged foxhole. As they did so hands would reach out from the ground and take food and ammunition from the stretcher, a clear violation of the Geneva Convention. They were also notorious for carrying ammunition and other forbidden objects in their ambulances. After the medics had moved on we waited for a half hour or so in order to obscure the fact that we had observed what was going on, then dropped mortar fire on each of the revealed foxholes in rather random order. I think they realized what they had done as the medics did not reappear. Live (if you're lucky) and learn.

The first night we were in Coin-sur-Seille the 10th Infantry attacked Pournoy la Chetive on our left. It was not far away and was the noisiest fire fight I ever heard. The din was deafening; Jerry used a lot of artillery and screaming meemies. Machine gun fire was constant; the German machine guns were easily distinguished from ours as they fired at 1200-1500 rounds a minute, the individual reports blending almost into one, in contrast to our machine guns which fired only about 500 rounds/ minute and had a slow distinct Bam, Bam, Bam sound. In addition Jerry ran tanks into the town, firing their machine guns and 88s while the 10th Infantry, which had no antitank defense aside from our shoulder mounted bazookas, suffered numerous casualties. At night the visual effects of the tracer fire from the machine guns and the rocket trail from the screaming meemies was spectacular. There were numerous counterattacks by both sides and the intense fighting continued all night and well into the next day.

The 2nd Battalion of the 10th Infantry bore the brunt of the fighting, was reinforced by C Company of the 10th, and held onto the town. I would add that the 10th Infantry had a very high percentage of regular army men in it and was an exceptionally outstanding unit. The enemy in this sector was the 17th SS Panzer Grenadier Division, a good one and one we ran into frequently.

Eventually, however, the 10th had to abandon the position on our left; the 7th Armored had never come up on our right and Jerry infiltrated troops behind us, cutting off communication with any friendly troops for several days. The situation was serious but could have been worse as we were able, at night, to sneak through the lightly held line they held to replenish our ammunition. We stuck it out there for four days in the rain, fighting off small scale counterattacks and enduring constant shelling, but our line was too long and thinly spread to continue in place and we had to fall back to Silligny on the 24th and relieve elements of the 7th Armored Division.

The withdrawal itself was almost an example of the blind leading the blind. We withdrew at night, I can recall no light being evident at all and there was a constant drizzle. Someone led the column, probably Lt. Murphy, and I assume he just took a compass bearing toward friendly lines and followed it. I could see nothing in the darkness, we simply held on to the pack of the man in front of us and followed blindly. There was the usual accordion movement with the column alternately stretching and compacting as we moved. Occasionally we would lose contact with the man in front of and had to struggle forward while the man behind held us back. There was no visual contact, if you lost touch with the man in front you were immediately disoriented and lost in space. How the man leading the column got us out I'll never know. At one point the man in front of me suddenly dropped and I fell down behind him, both of us stepping, or more accurately falling, into a steam which was about knee deep. The withdrawal took several hours though we probably didn't go more than a mile or two before we entered friendly lines. The Germans holding the line between us and the American lines were not evident, possibly just holed up trying to stay dry.

Static Warfare

Letter, October 16th-I'm doing OK now that I've put some new notches in my belt so that my pants stay up. I finally got a package Mom mailed in July. At this rate I may get a Christmas package by the 4th of July. Here's a social note forThe Licking Valley Courier.

"Pfc. Lawrence Nickell of West Liberty and Pfc Andrew Carpenter of Mt. Sterling are batching out the duration in a comfortable two man fox hole somewhere in France. This fox hole is complete with a log and dirt roof and running water (when it rains). Two fleas and a tick were guests the other night and dined on fresh blood from their hosts. Carpenter and Nickell called for an artillery mission and blasted them out. For bravery above and beyond the call of duty Carpenter was awarded the Silver Spoon with an Oatmeal Cluster. Sgt. Orvel Chaney, of Chapel, Ky., will be a guest tonite and will be served a delicious cold K ration."

I see the troops stationed in Paris won't have any hot water in their hotels once the remnants of German coal run out. Tsk!Tsk! The hardships they must endure. I see one of my classmates is home on furlough again. He must wear horse shoes instead of dog tags.

The climate over here should be very healthful from now on. All the germs froze to death last night. I tried to wash my face this morning but couldn't get enough water. They say cleanliness is next to Godliness, I say it's next to impossible.

We occupied some high ground east of the Moselle overlooking German positions south of Metz. The usual disposition of the battalion in a static position was with two rifle companies on line facing the enemy and one in reserve. Initially A Company was in reserve in a valley behind the high ground where we set up reserve positions, digging foxholes and covering them with logs and dirt for protection against tree bursts as the position was in the woods. Some made use of German empty wooden shell boxes, filling them with dirt and constructing above the ground dug outs which were drier than regular foxholes. We were called on to make reconnaissance patrols, made up off four or five men. They were usually relatively noneventful but still rather stressful even though we seldom went more than a few hundred yards from our outpost lines. Occasionally a combat patrol went out with the express purpose of taking prisoners, *very* stressful!

After a few days in reserve we took over C Company's position on the front line. On this occasion our mortar section was dug in in a clearing in a forest on a hill several hundred feet behind the rifle platoons. We had time to dig elaborate bunkers. Andy and I dug a hole about five feet deep and six or eight feet square and covered it with logs, then with three or four feet of dirt which gave protection from anything but a direct hit by a large caliber artillery shell. The holes were lined with empty sand bags to keep the dirt from crumbling in on us. Shelter halves were placed on top of the dirt to divert rain and then foliage was placed on that to camouflage the area. We used a canteen filled with gasoline wicked with a sock as a lantern; the light was poor and there was a lot of smoke but it was bright enough to let us read the paperback pocket books the armed forces provided. My favorites were the Kenneth Roberts novels about the American Revolution. We dug an eight or ten foot square hole for platoon headquarters and played poker or black jack in it on occasion. The holes gave us protection from the cold frosty nights of October and were snug and dry.

For a while life was easy. The nights were cold and frosty but the days, if sunny, were pleasant and we could sit near the entrance of our holes and read. We had two hot meals a day, K rations for dinner and an occasional 10 in 1 ration for variety. The hot food came up by jeep in insulated Marmac cans and we sometimes got mail with the evening meal. Relatively speaking, life was good. We had a dry place to sleep, adequate food and relative safety. For the short term I couldn't have asked for more and an infantryman really shouldn't develop a long term outlook.

There was relatively little combat activity for us at this time. We had few firing missions, there was little aggressive action by either the Germans or by us. Duty while we were on the front was not very arduous, usually consisting of spending a few hours on the phone in the platoon command post while Trigger, Judge, Chaney or Herman Heath manned the forward observation post. We fired a little on most days, usually one gun at a time zeroing in on possible future target areas. At night we would lay a gun over a front line platoon area, each situated so that we could fire a parachute flare to illuminate the area in front of each platoon.

We received less artillery fire in the forward positions than in the reserve positions but some positions received direct hits and there were more casualties. One outstanding event that I recall occurred while we were in reserve was the shelling that we took from a sixteen inch railroad gun. Our kitchen was set up in a valley which could not be observed by the enemy. One midday when we were in reserve the company was lined up for lunch, with men spaced at eight or ten foot intervals to minimize possible casualties, when there was a tremendous roar which sounded like multiple high speed trains coming in. The shell stuck twenty or thirty feet from the chow line and buried up a good bit in the soft ground but it was a dud and produced no casualties though it dug a hole four by ten feet across. The sixteen inch railroad gun was in the city of Metz, hidden in a tunnel when it was not firing, and was eventually neutralized by bombing the entrances of the tunnel sealing the gun inside.

There was a good bit of German aerial activity during the time we were there. This consisted primarily of reconnisance overflights, sometimes followed shortly by brief but intense artillery fire. There were several hits close to our hole but the logs and dirt covering the holes prevented any injury.

We were baffled by relatively accurate fire falling in an area not observable by the enemy but a few nights after the sixteen inch shelling a civilian was detected signaling the Germans with a flashlight and was, I understand, summarily executed. The province of Lorraine had been switched back and forth between France and Germany on several occasions and was incorporated into Germany, most recently in 1940 after the blitzkreig. The street signs were in German and German was the language in the schools. Many of the people in the area were pro German so that it was not surprising that there were a number of spies in the area.

One night we were alerted for a possible attack by a propaganda loudspeaker broadcast from the German lines, calling us to surrender and spend Christmas in Berlin. They said we were surrounded, that Private Wood of the 11th Infantry had been captured and revealed all our positions and that at daylight the mighty German army would attack and destroy us. We concluded that we would prefer a diet of K rations to one of sauerkraut and stayed put.

After several pleasant days in this area we were relieved on October 16th by the 378th Infantry Regiment, 95th Infantry Division, which was coming on line for combat duty for the first time. Their vehicles had been used in the Red Ball Express operation for some time but they were now freed up for combat duty. I recall one of their sergeants commenting that he was afraid that the war would be over before he could see any combat. The 95th had a very important role to play in the upcoming Metz campaign and I'm sure he got all the combat he wanted. The relief was carried out at night as was usually the case, the relieving company taking over our positions. We left our mortars, which had been preregistered on enemy targets, exchanging them with the mortars of our relieving companies so that they could fire on known targets without having to find the range and azimuth anew.

It was an exhausting march out, recrossing the Moselle with the usual stop and start rhythm of a night march. It was muddy, as usual. and when we reached the point where we were to load on trucks we all simply collapsed in the mud of the ditches. Lieutenant Murphy, who was acting as company commander as usual, was one of the most exhausted looking humans I have ever seen. Usually as immaculate as one can look in a rifle company, his clothes were covered with mud, his pants hung out of his leggings as he walked along the line checking his men. He had been acting as company commander since the beginning of the Loiville attack and was worn out.

The company was moved up near the Belgian border to Morfontaine, a former French military base. An Air Force engineering unit was stationed there but we were quartered in barracks and were allowed access to showers one time while we were there. There was a movie every night but the engineers filled the hall most nights before we finished our training. We had the first day free to clean up and write letters but after that we began training at 1300 hours (1 P M). We trained on assault tactics against fixed field fortifications (pillboxes etc.) of the Maginot line (the French defensive forts facing to the east, a classic example of the futility of a defensive rather thanan offensive philosophy). We handled demolitions, blew up embrasures (the firing slots) on pillboxes, used flame throwers etc. The mortar section fired a good bit in these training exercises. We came in at 1800 hours (6PM), ate supper and went back out on night problems until three AM, ate breakfast and went to bed. It rained during the time we were in Morfontaine and every one was disgusted at having to lie out in the rain all night just to satisfy the brass hat's need to keep us busy.The assault training was probably useful but the night training was strictly eye wash.

During the training we were briefed on the Metz fortifications and given updates on the front line situation in general. One night we had a beer party but no one liked the Belgian beer and we went to bed early. We did play a little poker and Lt. Ives, acting as our platoon leader at the time, shared his liquor ration of two fifths a month with us, the only platoon leader of five I had while with A Company to do so. He had been in combat in the Pacific as a sergeant and probably had a bit different outlook than most of the others.

On the last day of October we left Morfontaine, were driven back to the Moselle and took up billets in the little village of Vittonville on the east bank of the river.

October 22nd-I can't complain, I'm free, white though not yet 21 but, most important, I'm still alive. I'm glad to hear Bernard Hill is out of Jerry's hands. (Bernard was a classmate shot down at Ploesti and liberated from a Bulgarian prison camp by the Russians.)

Vittionville

If any question why we died,
Tell them, because our fathers lied.

Epitaphs of the War
Rudyard Kipling

The weapons platoon was billeted in the cellar of a stone house in the village of Vittionville over looking the Moselle valley. We stayed there for eight days, training for assault river crossings, going down to the river in the afternoon and at night, carrying assault boats down to the river, paddling across and assuming positions on the "enemy" bank. As a matter of information the Fifth Division made more assault river crossings than any other unit in Europe. Patton, in a letter written to the division after the war, commented that he was convinced that we had webbed feet as a result of the many river crossings. In addition we had classes on enemy weapons and military tactics.

While we were in Vitionville the presidential elections were being held in the States. The Stars and Stripes had several editorials stating that all the men in the front lines were anxious to see Roosevelt reelected. We got a kick out of this as very few of us cared at all who was elected. We had little interest in politics or in current events in general; our perspective was limited, by and large, to the life and death events on the front line. The only comments I can recall about the election were sarcastic comments about politicians who send other men to die. This was especially the case in the Fifth Division as the old timers had been shipped to Europe in September of 1941, in spite of Roosevelt's pledge in 1940 that "No American boy will ever set foot on foreign soil." The division, in the fall of 1944, had been overseas for three years and there were already relatively few of the old timers left in the rifle companies. A few had gone back as cadre for new units being formed but many fought and died without seeing their loved ones for over three years. There were no furloughs or rotations home at this time though, in late November or so, the Army did initiate a policy of rotating a few men with the longest overseas time home. Long overdue!

At about this time the United Mine Workers were striking for higher wages and some of the defense plants had to shut down as a result of a coal shortage. We would have been glad to make our point with the strikers- the point of a bayonet. At the time there was a shortage of artillery shells and we needed all the artillery support we could get.

In Vittionville we had three hot meals a day and a fair amount of time to ourselves for letter writing and reading. We felt that the training was appropriate and useful with a minimum of the usual "chickenshit" which was often imposed in training just to keep us occupied. Our quarters were dry and we were content with our situation, which we knew was about to end.

On one occasion the officers and platoon sergeants of the division were taken back to hear Patton give a speech. It was, as usual, rather colorful and blunt. During the speech he said that the Fifth was one of the best divisions in the army, the only complaint he had about us was that we didn't use enough ammunition. He also said "If you think you're going to sit on your ass in the mud all winter you're crazy. You're going to attack Christmas day. And if that son of a bitch Roosevelt can change Thanksgiving day I can change the date of Christmas."As we subsequently learned his Christmas came on November 9th. In case anyone reading this is confused about the Thanksgiving comment Roosevelt changed the Thanksgiving date, which classically was the last Thursday in November, to an earlier date in the hope of spreading holiday spending over a longer period of time as an economic measure.

At this time my personal attitude toward the war was as follows. "If I survive it unscathed, well and good. If I am wounded I may get to go home, which is good. If I am killed I may go to heaven, which will be wonderful. If I am killed and go to hell it can't be any worse than infantry combat."

On the evening of November 8th Lt. Ives came down to our billet with maps and a notebook. We knew from his expression that the big attack on Metz was to get underway soon and that we were to play a major role with an expected high casualty rate. He briefed us on what we were expected to do. The attack was to come off early the next morning and we were to leave Vittionville at 0130 hours (1:30 AM). Breakfast was to be served just before that and it was to be our last hot meal for at least a week.

Church services were held, almost everyone went. The statement that there are no atheists in foxholes is profoundly true. The belief in a benevolent God was, and is, the single greatest sustaining factor in my life and in the lives of most of us.

We packed up our bed rolls which we had not seen much of, as they were only available when we were quartered in buildings. They contained extra uniforms, blankets and personal items which we could not carry in combat. Combat packs were made up, all unnecessary items disposed of and we wrote what would be, for many, last letters home. We came back to the cellar and sat and smoked, waiting. No one slept, I smoked four packs of cigarettes in about twelve hours, looked at the floor and prayed, wondering how many of us would be alive the next night. With every heart beat I seemed to hear a voice, relentlessly and ever louder, saying "It's coming, it's coming, it's coming, nearer, nearer."

Davis, the section runner, who was from a small town in Arkansas, the father of several children, who really should not have been in a combat situation, had a harmonica. He lay on the floor in the straw and played "Home, Sweet Home" and other nostalgic songs over and over again. There is a description in Shelby Foote's narrative of the battle of Stone's River describing the bands in the Confederate and Union armies playing Home, Sweet Home in unison the night before the battle. Things don't change a great deal. However this time I didn't hear Jerry playing with Davis. Maybe they didn't have harmonicas.

It was dark, the only light from a flickering single candle made everything seem like a dream, the figment of some insane mind. It was beyond doubt the worst run up to a battle that I can recall, probably because we were attacking the Metz fortifications again after previous heavy losses, and because we had spent a few days away from the front line in a quiet situation, and knew what lay ahead of us. As a rule, we had little forewarning of the resistance we might encounter on any given day and took each day as we came to it. There was little point in worrying about danger; nothing happens until it happens and worry does not help. A given day might be good or bad but anticipation was pointless. Hemingway in *Men at War* states that learning to suspend your imagination and to live completely in the very second of the present minute with no before or after is the greatest gift a soldier can acquire. It probably is a good general philosophy for everyone. In the case of the upcoming attacks we knew what we faced and it was impossible to ignore.

At 0130 hours , after an early breakfast of hot cakes, bacon and coffee, we began the march to the line of departure.

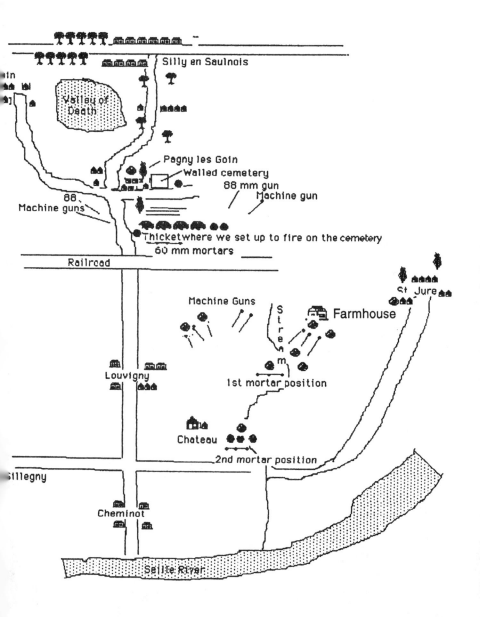

Silly en Saulnois

Valley of Death

Pagny les Goin

Walled cemetery

88 mm gun

Machine gun

88

Machine guns

Thicket where we set up to fire on the cemetery

60 mm mortars

Railroad

Machine Guns

Stream

Farmhouse

1st mortar position

Louvigny

Chateau

2nd mortar position

St Jure

Sillegny

Cheminot

Selite River

"Attack"

I hate that drum's discordant sound,
Parading round, and round, and round:
To me it talks of ravaged plains,
And burning towns, and ruined swains,
And mangled limbs and dying groans,
And widow's tears, and orphan's moans:
And all that misery's hand bestows,
To fill the catalogue of human woes.

The Drum
John Scott of Amwell

As we moved out of Vittionville on the approach march the nervousness and fear began to drop away and a feeling of confidence grew. We walked through the night south along the Moselle valley, then turned to the east, crossed a hill and dropped down into the valley of the Seille River, a tributary of the Moselle . It was a moonlit night with occasional clouds scudding across the face of the moon and, with the exception of the sound of distant artillery fire, it was surprisingly quiet. There was no massive preparatory artillery barrage. The Moselle and Seille valleys were flooded, the worst flood in seventy years, and I suspect the preliminary barrage was held off in the expectation that the Germans would not anticipate an attack under those conditions. As we left the road and began to move cross country into a wood, which was the First Battalion assembly point , daylight began to break.

The plan of attack was for the Second Battalion to effect a river crossing and to take the town of Cheminot which lay on the high ground immediately to the front of the crossing. We were to push through them and take Louvigny and the high ground north of St. Jure. All of these were small villages, made up of the usual stone farmhouses and barns built around central barn yards, ideal minifortresses. We moved out soon after the Second Battalion had made the Seille River crossing, apparently with little resistance and few casualties. The river, in flood, was about a hundred and fifty yards wide. A causeway ran across the river but had been partially blown; the Seventh Engineers had thrown foot bridges across the gaps. As we began to cross the river Jerry threw in several screaming meemies which were short of the mark and no one was injured. After we crossed the river we swung to the right, following the Seille for several hundred yards, then pushed up a long open valley of one of the river's tributaries.

The terrain was open and rolling and, as a result of the heavy rains, the ground was soft, muddy and very difficult to walk in. At every step the mud would ooze up over our boot tops. We walked through a mine field soon after crossing the river. No one was injured as the ground was soaked and the mines did not detonate.

We moved up on the high ground to our right, keeping below the skyline, and moving along at a slow steady pace, meeting no resistance. As we moved we passed several pillboxes which were not occupied. They faced to the east rather than the west, the direction we were coming from, having been built by the French to defend against the Germans coming from the east. Troops of the 80th Division could be seen moving along on our right and we could see P-47s strafing and dive bombing positions ahead of us. B-17 and B-25 bombers flew over in a steady stream, visible on this sunny day with only scattered cloud cover, striking targets behind the German lines. The path finder flares they dropped were clearly visible. We could hear the rumble of the bombs as they struck. It was the largest aerial show we had seen since Normandy and the largest combined air-ground operation that I personally took part in. So far it was deceptively easy.

The first resistance we hit was in the form of incoming artillery fire. We were attacking in battalion column formation with A Company on the point, that is the leading company. The battalion was well dispersed and the artillery fire caused few casualties. Andy and I were moving along fairly close together when we heard incoming artillery that obviously was targeted to hit very close to us. Three shells struck- Zip! Zip! Zip!,-within ten to fifteen feet of us. They formed a triangle with the two of us in the center but all were duds, possibly failing to detonate because of the deep soft mud where they struck. We hit the dirt as soon as we realized they were on target, we being the target, but moved away from the area as fast as possible as more would probably be coming into the column at that point.

Cloud cover began moving in about ten that morning and it began to spit a little snow, the first snowfall of the year. The column stopped as we made contact with the 80th Division and I broke out a K ration and began to eat.

As we moved out again we passed an old chateau which sat on the edge of a stream. A bridge crossing the stream had been blown and a platoon of light tanks which was supposed to support us was unable to cross to our side. We were on the north side of the stream, the tanks on the hilly south side. As we moved forward they too advanced but the terrain prevented their giving us constant supporting fire. There were trees on our right to the south which sheltered us to some extent from observation from the south but as we emerged from their cover the lead platoon became engaged in a fire fight with a small enemy force on high ground on our right. The column halted, everyone stood in place and looked around, sky gazing to some extent at the P-47s overhead. I noted a dead German soldier on the far side of the stream to my right but had no sooner seen him than all hell broke loose. Enemy machine gun fire came lacing through the column from both flanks and from the front. It was especially heavy coming from a stone farmhouse on a hill to our right front. We had casualties with the first burst of fire, everyone hit the ground where he stood. I had on a packboard of eighteen rounds of 60 mm. mortar ammunition which I slipped off as quickly as possible and then crawled over to seek visual shelter behind some bushes on the stream bank.

The fire grew more intense as we took up the fire fight. Tracers were snapping and popping through the bushes a foot or so over my head and dirt was being kicked up by enemy fire all through the field. Davis, Burghett and Wally Pryzdraga lay where they were when the fight started. Davis was hit several times in the back and Burghett in the hand. Wally lifted his head to look around and two bullets ricocheted off of his helmet, knocking his face into the ground but failing to penetrate his helmet. Herman Heath started across the stream to take shelter under the far bank but it was over his head and he almost drowned before he got across. Our machine gun squads tried to deploy on the far side of the stream but would have lost both guns had it not been for Bucher, a gunner who was about six- six, who was able to wade across holding the guns overhead.

The Third Platoon deployed to the high ground to the north but their added fire did not silence Jerry. Sgt. Pierce, who was with the Third Platoon at the time, called for Sgt. Ramicone to start a withdrawal. The light tanks accompanying us had opened up on the farmhouse but two of them had been knocked out by 88s and the others had to withdraw. Our artillery observer was unable, because of heavy fire, to get up to us and get a fix on enemy positions. He did call in several missions which had no effect.

Ramicone, who lay beside me, looked at me and said "Get a packboard and get the hell out of here." Just then a Second Platoon rifleman lying nearby was hit several times in the leg. I looked at him as he cried out for help but Ramicone said "God damn it, can't you understand the English language? Get going!" I got up, grabbed a packboard and started running for the cover of the trees. It was about sixty yards to the trees and I could see men in front of me trying to get across the stream to cover. The air seemed filled with white tracers which poured into the small space we had to cross the fordable area of the stream. Men would get up in front of me, head toward the trees and, as a string of tracers would pass through them, fell to the ground or into the stream. I started to dive into the stream on my left but realized that the heavy packboard would drown me. I kept running and jumped across the stream at the narrow point and fell flat on my face, rose and moved to a sheltered point behind a small hill. The rest of the company withdrew to the same area and we started to dig in. Enemy artillery began to fall in the area but was rather inaccurate and we had few casualties from it.

As we dug in the third squad gun Ramicone called Wally, Russ, Stamper, Shanks and me over and told us to come with him to get some tubes of mortar ammunition left where we hit the initial resistance. We were limited in the amount of mortar fire we could deliver by the weight and bulk of the shells; only nine men in the mortar section carried pack boards and, for this attack, many of the riflemen had been given one tube of six mortar shells to carry. They dropped them on hitting resistance, as planned, and we were to retrieve them.

Everything was quiet as we crossed the stream and crawled along by the sheltering bushes. The nearest tubes of ammunition were about thirty feet from us. Ramicone signaled for Wally to go out and get a tube. He picked one up and not a shot was fired. I walked out as Wally started to pick up a second one and Jerry opened up. I grabbed a tube under each arm and started running toward the stream with machine gun fire kicking up the dirt around me. I felt something slap one of the tubes under my arm as tracers passed through the space between my arm and body but I held on to it until I got back across the stream. I threw both tubes on the ground and started cursing Lt. Ives for ordering us to go into the field and retrieve the tubes. However, when I looked at the tubes and saw that one of them had been hit three times, I thought about how lucky I was and shut up. The impact of the bullets should have detonated the shells. There would have been nothing left of me to bury. There is no reasonable explanation for the failure of them to detonate unless, by some miraculous quirk, the bullets hit only the heavy cardboard of the tube and not the shells inside.

We dug in while B and C Companies moved out of the valley and attacked Louvigny which lay to the front and to our left. They took it as darkness fell and the Third Battalion came up and took over our positions. My platoon spent the night in a barn at the chateau we had passed earlier, the floor was covered with manure but we were out of the sleet and sleeping in cow manure was no worse than sleeping in the mud and sleet outside.

Baron Marbot, a French officer in the Napoleonic wars, wrote of having to sleep in the manure of a barn during a winter campaign. He was of a lower rank than a Field Marshall and had to sleep near the door where it was colder than the interior where the Marshall was. Except for the weapons war probably has changed little for ground troops since that time.

Before daylight the next morning we moved through Louvigny preparing to attack Pagny les Goin. The morning of November 9th we had 200-210 fighting men in the company; the next morning we had about 180 left in the company. We had been able to fire only one gun in the mortar section because definite targets were hard to spot and the enemy fire was so intense that we were unable to set the guns up.

Pagny les Goin

"You are not a soldier until you realize you are going to die."
James Jones-WW II

As daylight came we moved through Louvigny which was badly torn up. It had been shelled for more than a month and the preparatory barrage before the final assault had been terrific. B and C Companies had carried on an intensive fire fight in the village with many casualties on both sides. As we moved through the town Wally and Russ rejoined us; they had been separated from the company during the move in the night. The ground was soft, muddy and full of craw fish holes. I noted that the grass was similar, if not identical, to the sedge grass in America. It continued to spit snow but the sun occasionally broke through. Our objective was Pagny les Goin, a village which was a mile or so to the east. There were only a few houses and barns in the village but there was a walled cemetery which was, in essence, a small fortress with well entrenched troops who punched holes in the walls of the cemetery. We were not initially aware of that, however.

We moved across a railroad track which had deep ditches on either side, ideal for mortar positions. A battlefield can be a strange, empty looking place. You know there are enemy troops watching you advance but there may be no sign of them until they open fire. As we started across an open field, approaching the village, we noticed a German in a long overcoat about 500 yards away walking slowly across a cabbage field. No one fired at him. We knew he had seen us but he was in no hurry. He eventually got into a foxhole and opened up on us with a machine gun. As soon as he fired we began receiving fire from both flanks and from the front.

We ran across an open field as rapidly as possible and took cover behind a small thicket. On the far side of the thicket there was a small vineyard where two of our rifle platoons were pinned down. Another of the rifle platoons deployed to our left and B and C Companies came up and deployed to the left of A Company. Some Third Battalion troops were attacking about 500 yards to our right, moving steadily through a hail of mortar and artillery fire. The fire fight in front of us grew in intensity but we were unable to advance because of fire from Germans in the walled cemetery to our front and from a ravine on our left.

We set up our mortars behind the thicket and began firing on the cemetery without digging in, the need for fire taking precedence over safety. O' Conner and I opened up and expended all of the ammunition in our squad, then began using the first and second squad's ammunition. Herman Heath, who was our squad leader at the time, still wet and cold from his attempt to cross the stream the day before, tried to heat up a cup of coffee as we fired. After we had fired a few rounds artillery fire began to zero in on our position and we had to take cover in a ditch near the thicket between fire missions. Some light tanks came up near us and the incoming artillery fire intensified. We continued to fire the Third Squad mortar and succeeded in knocking out two machine guns and killing several riflemen but some of the enemy in the cemetery were too well dug in and continued to hold us up. Lt. Horn attempted to rush the place but was killed by a head shot. Lt. Murphy led a small group of men around the cemetery and came in from the flank, killing several Germans and capturing the rest. The resistance on the left began to crumble and the fire fight moved on into the village. As this fight developed tanks and half tracks of the Sixth Armored Division began moving along our right flank with the object of capturing Vigny which lay to our right front. Jerry switched his artillery fire from us to the armored troops on our right. We lay and watched the armor moving up and, as we looked to our rear, we could see flashes from our artillery pieces pounding German positions. They had displaced forward with our advance.

A Long, Dark, Bad Afternoon

Half a league, half a league,
Half a league onward,
All in the Valley of Death
Rode the six hundred.
"Forward the Light Brigade!
Charge for the guns!" he said.
Into the Valley of Death
Rode the six hundred.

The Charge of the Light Brigade-*Tennyson*

No,we weren't on horseback but there were about six hundred of us left in the battalion and it was as close to the Valley of Death as A Company will ever come. And the mud made the charge a very slow one.

About 1300 hours we finally cleared the town of Pagny les Goin of enemy troops and moved through the hamlet, preparing to attack Silly en Saulnois to the east. We dug in to the east of the village and reorganized preparatory to the next attack. The ammo bearers went back to the ammo point and replenished our supply of shells. A Company, which had the point in the morning, reverted to battalion reserve and we moved out, B and C Companies in parallel columns and A Company in single column behind them.

It had been cloudy all morning with rain falling intermittently and the ground was very soft and muddy. We passed through wheat and freshly plowed fields and the going, with the heavy loads we were bearing, was slow and tiresome as our feet sank ankle deep in the mud and the thick tenacious mud stuck to our feet, adding extra pounds to the burden we already carried. A company of tanks was supporting the battalion; a tank would occasionally bog down and others would have to pull it out. We moved down a shallow valley, then mounted a slight rise and crossed a road, passing an undefended cemetery as the village of Silly en Saulnois came into view a mile down a long slope to the front. The village of Goin lay apparently undefended to our left front. A platoon of tank destroyers, which were tracked vehicles similar to tanks but more lightly armored and with more powerful guns, moved into position on the crest of the rise as we passed it. A road perpendicular to our front ran through Silly in front of us and as we moved toward it German trucks, tanks and half tracks began to flee to the north down the tree lined road. The rifle companies ahead of us opened up on the fleeing column and the tanks began firing their 76 and 90 mm. guns as well as their machine guns at Jerry.

At the time A Company was moving along with the third and weapons platoon mixed in with the tanks which were separated from one another by thirty or forty yards. We did not set up our weapons as the enemy vehicles were under heavy fire already and moving too fast for mortar fire to be effective. One truck received a direct hit from a 76 mm. shell which just knocked it over and blew it to pieces. The tanks were a notorious as a preferential target for enemy fire and I had a strong premonition that we would be drawing fire. The tank tracks in the mud were almost knee deep and I moved over behind a tank and began walking in the deep furrowed track. We had been receiving light small arms fire but suddenly all hell broke loose. Due to the noise of the tank fire around us, we were unable to hear incoming artillery fire and a barrage of 100 mm. artillery, 120 mm. mortar and 88 mm. antipersonnel shells, both air burst and impact-detonating fire, as well as machine gun fire, hit us without warning. The first indication any of us had was the explosion of shells around us. The first indication I had was a black puff of smoke in front of me and a concussion which knocked me flat on my back in the tank track.

The weapons platoon and the third platoon took most of the brunt of the barrage. I slipped the packboard off my back and moved as deeply into the track as possible. China wouldn't have been deep enough. I felt blood trickling down my face and pulled a small sliver of shrapnel no larger than a dime from my right cheek, which was beginning to swell. I looked at Stamper, who was lying next to me, and asked him if there was much of a cut on my face. He looked at me for a moment, groaned and said "No". I saw that he had blood on his back and, as I got up to see if I could help him, saw that Trigger, Ramicone, Herman Heath, Mike Robers, Pat Halloran , George O'Conner and a new mortar section runner, whose name I don't recall, had been hit. 20 mm. tracers were crackling overhead but the artillery barrage moved forward from our position following the tanks and began falling on B and C Companies. The 20 mm. fire was too high to be effective and some continuing air burst incoming artillery was also too high. Most of the men in the Third Platoon were hit. There was a large bomb crater to our right front and medics were working on casualties there while others took shelter there from enemy fire.

Aid men were attached to each rifle company, during an attack there may have been one attached to each rifle platoon, but they were overwhelmed by the number of casualties. In addition, some aid men usually followed us up with stretchers but the mud and distance permitted only a few men to be borne back to the aid station before dark.

In the midst of all this havoc Lt. Colonel Blakefield, the battalion commander, came striding through, oblivious to the sporadic incoming fire and intent on taking of the village before us before dark.

Murany, Shanks, Russ Miller, Andy and I started doing what we could for the wounded in the platoon. Wally and Rosenal cracked up. Rosenal went back toward Pagny but Wally couldn't move, he just lay on the ground and sobbed. Russ and I worked on Stamper and Ramicone while Shanks and Murany went to see what they could do for Trigger but he was dead, his back and legs raked by shrapnel. Mike Robers was also dead. I don't know what happened to the section runner. O'Conner had been hit by shrapnel from 20 mm. fire but was not seriously injured. Stamper was hit in the buttock and Ramicone in the small of the back. We did what we could for them; bandaged their wounds, sprinkled sulfa powder in the wounds and gave them sulfa tablets. We took blankets and shelter halves from the packs of the dead , wrapped the wounded up as best we could and rolled them into the tank tracks for protection against sporadic incoming fire. Shanks and I tried to get Wally to his feet but he didn't want to move. We finally dragged him to his feet and half carried him until he started to walk a little.

We then started back toward the aid station with Wally, a man from the Third Platoon with a back and buttock wound, Pat Halloran who was hit in the face, and Herman Heath who had been hit in the throat. As we moved back toward Pagny les Goin we passed observers from the 50th Field Artillery and some tank destroyers who were covering our advance. The sun came out for a few moments and we stopped and rested on some hay bales. Shock was beginning to wear off Wally and he walked along slowly. He and Pat Halloran were simply too old to be in a rifle company. Pat was 38 and I'm not sure how old Wally was but infantry combat is a young man's game. Wally had a narrow escape the day before, when a bullet hit his helmet and glanced off, and he had fallen the night before, briefly being knocked out.

We found the Aid Station in a cellar in Pagny les Goin and Shanks and I went in to see about getting more medics out into the field. Captain Selter, the battalion surgeon, sent us out with two jeeps rigged with stretchers but they bogged down a few hundred yards from Pagny. We went back and got a Weasel, which was a low open tracked vehicle, but it too bogged down in the mud, only slightly further than the jeep had gone. The litter squad leader refused to walk out to the wounded, he said it was about two miles and that it would be impossible to carry the wounded that far in the deep mud. He was probably right but I was very angry about it. We went back to the aid station and waited for any new reports. Some of the tanks were coming back in to refuel, bringing in some of the wounded but none of the men in our section.

A little after dark we met Murany and Andy so there was little point in going back out, the weapons platoon was, in effect, gone. I understood Lt. Ives had either been wounded or had cracked up the day before and the section sergeant and squad leaders were dead or wounded, there was no hope of finding the mortars in the dark. Of the seventeen men in the mortar section four were killed, five were wounded and two were evacuated for battle fatigue. The section, in effect, ceased to exist as a combat unit at that time.

Duane Kinman, a medic attached to D Company, had come back into the aid station that night after checking Ramicone and Stamper. He had done an emergency tracheotomy in the late evening. A soldier had been wounded in the throat with obstruction of his airway and the medic had made an incision into his trachea and used the outer sheath of a fountain pen, which he slipped into his trachea, as a tube to keep his airway open. The field medics were enlisted men who really had limited training but did a great job and probably got more Congressional Medals of Honor proportionately than any other single group. Duane got a scholarship to Western Reserve Medical School for that as well, I suppose, as his general high standards.

At daylight the next morning Shanks, and I started back up to find the company. We ran into a jeep driver from the company who gave us a cup of hot coffee. As we walked toward Silly en Saulnois we ran into an artillery observer who let us look through his scope at the town of Metz, the first time I had seen it. Shanks' feet were hurting him and he turned himself into the aid station with trench foot. I caught a ride up to the company. Schmitt, the company radio man, told me that Ramicone had been evacuated but that Stamper had died during the night, probably from blood loss, shock and exposure. The medics who wouldn't walk out were across the street from me and I started crying and cursing them and myself for letting Stamper lie out in the mud and cold and die. Schmitt made me lie down and put a blanket over me. Lt. Murphy came by and I told him where I had seen Andy and the remnant of the platoon last. He put me in a jeep and sent me to the aid station. Oddly enough the evacuation slip tied on me recorded that I had entered the aid station at 11 A. M. November 11th, the time the guns ceased fire in the First World War. By that time my cheek where the shrapnel and mud had hit me was swollen so that I could no longer open my right eye. I was evacuated to a clearing station where the wounded were evaluated for the type of treatment they would require, then sent to the 34th Evacuation Hospital in Verdun where I stayed for two or three days. In the hospital I saw Sgt. Ramicone, who was sent on back to a General Hospital for more intensive care, and I also heard that Lt. Ives. was there in the hospital though I didn't get to see him and do not know what happened to him.

A Company had gone from about 220 men, being somewhat over strength on November 8th, to fewer than 30 men on November 11th, the second time in sixty days we had been hit that hard. According to the regimental history the 1st Battalion experienced it's most terrible wounds of the war in that attack on November 10th. The Metz operation was undoubtedly the most difficult one we participated in. Subsequent operations were no bed of roses but we never again met such bitter resistance for such a sustained period of time.

The swelling on my face subsided rapidly, I had an interview with a Major Majors (same name as in the book Catch 22) who asked if I was ready to go back to the front and I could see no valid reason to say no provided I went back to A Company. He sent me back after giving me a Purple Heart, which I sent home. The Purple Heart is a medal which is given when a serviceman is wounded or killed.

The closest relative of a serviceman was notified by telegram when he was killed or wounded. I entered service from a small town, knew the phone operators who received the telegrams well and had arranged for them to notify my brother Blaine, first rather than my parents as Dad was in poor health and I thought it best that Blaine would convey the message rather than an impersonal piece of paper. A type of phone service we will never see again.

I have the Western Union message, hand written, that was delivered to Blaine.

November 12th-I want to get this off as soon as possible. By now you probably have received a telegram stating that I have been wounded in action. I wasn't hit bad, just a piece of shrapnel from an 88, just below my right eye. It gave me a good black eye and a small laceration. My eye swelled shut. It's ironic that I reported into the aid station at 11 AM, November 11th but it isn't over this time.

I'm going back to duty today. I suppose you've heard about the push, I can't say much about it but we're moving right along now. There are plenty of dead Krauts, that's how they all should be.

CLASS OF SERVICE DESIRED

DOMESTIC	CABLE
TELEGRAM	ORDINARY
DAY LETTER	URGENT RATE
SERIAL	DEFERRED
NIGHT LETTER	NIGHT LETTER

Patrons should check class of service desired; otherwise the message will be transmitted as a telegram or ordinary cablegram.

Charge to the account of _____ $ _____

WESTERN UNION

1206

A. N. WILLIAMS
PRESIDENT

CHECK

ACCOUNTING INFORMATION

TIME FILED
150 PM

Send the following telegram, subject to the terms on back hereof, which are hereby agreed to   April 5-45

FOR VICTORY
BUY
WAR BONDS
TODAY

Washington D.C.
Silas M. Nickell
West Liberty Ky

The Secretary of War desires me to express
his deep regret that your son Pfc Lawrence
A. Nickell was slightly wounded in Germany
24 March 1945. Continue to address mail to
him as formerly or until new address is
received from him.

J. A. Ulio
The Adjutant General

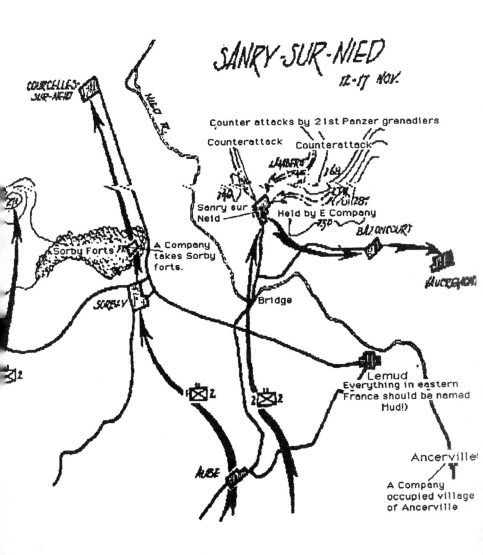

SANRY-SUR-NIED
12-17 NOV.

COURCELLES-SUR-NIED

Counter attacks by 21st Panzer grenadiers

Counterattack   Counterattack   Counterattack

Sanry sur Neid

Held by E Company

BAZONCOURT

Sorby Forts

A Company takes Sorby forts.

SORBY

Bridge

Lemud
Everything in eastern France should be named Mud!)

AUBE

Ancerville!

A Company occupied village of Ancerville

Ancerville and Fort Sorby

It ain't the guns or armament, or the money they can pay,
It's the close cooperation that makes them win the day:
It ain't the individual, it's the army as a whole
By the everlasting teamwork of every lasting soul.

J. Mason Knox- Cooperation

I spent a day or so in the 17th Replacement Depot in Verdun, an old French military post of brick barracks and a central courtyard. The "Repo Depos", as they were called, were simply holding areas for new men or returning wounded on the way to the front. In view of the cold, damp weather and the impersonal attitude of the permanent personnel there, I was glad to be shipped back to A Company.

I would comment here that the thing that keeps a soldier going in the face of horrendous violence and unbelievable (to 20th century Americans) living conditions is simply self respect and the psychological need for the respect of your fellow soldiers. You want them to support you when you are pinned down or in a bad spot and they need to feel that they can count on you. John Keegan comments in his book "*The Face of War*" that modern combat conditions are such that few men can psychologically stand more than three months of modern combat. Yet we had a lot of men who came back up after being wounded on several occasions, their only request being that they return to their old unit even though they knew there were only a few, in some cases none, of their old comrades. Call it esprit de corps or what have you, it gives men the backbone to survive. We had a lot of propaganda thrown at us about the cause for which we fought, and it was a good cause, but it was not as important as the morale of the unit and the respect that men had for one another.

I found the company in the woods east of Silly en Saulnois . We had a new platoon leader, Lt. Dahlrymple, who had been an attorney in civilian life. Orville Chaney, who had missed the recent action as a result of hospitalization with pneumonia, was back and a short, dark, droll, little fellow named Bombard had returned to the company after being wounded in Normandy. Pat Halloran also returned and there were new replacements. I don't recall all their names but Hoover, Covington, Grogan and Crutchfield I do recall. Another was a sergeant we called Zeke, I don't recall his proper name, Zackowski or something close to that. He was an old timer in the company but had been wounded in Normandy and had just come back up. We had a new company commander, a Captain Flynn, who lasted only a few days. In all, we had seven different company commanders.

We spent the night that I returned dug into the snow covered ground and moved out the next day to Ancerville, a village a bit further to the east. The encirclement of Metz was nearly complete and the Germans were trying to break out to the east. There was an intact bridge over the Neid River near the village which we were detailed to hold. The mortars were set up in the courtyard of a farmhouse and we quartered in the vaulted stone cellar, secure from just about any type of enemy fire. The Germans were attempting to retake the bridges in order to escape the encirclement and we caught a lot of artillery fire. They sent some rather vigorous patrols toward the town and the bridge which we were anxious to hold as a bridgehead for the Sixth Armored Division attack toward Germany.

While we were there the German 21st Panzer Grenadier Division violently attacked B and E Companies at Sanry sur Neid, which was adjacent to another bridge Jerry needed to escape from the encirclement of Metz. During a night attack they lost over two hundred dead and a hundred wounded when they broke into the village. American tanks in the village depressed their gun muzzles and fired shrapnel and machine guns into the road immediately in front of the tanks, sweeping the streets, and the American infantry in the houses fired rifle and machine gun fire at the tanks to keep the Germans from climbing on them. We had twenty two wounded, no dead and the bridge was held.

On the morning of the seventeenth of November the First Battalion attacked Fort Sorby which was one of the smaller forts to the east of Metz. It consisted mostly of rather large pillboxes and a good bit of barbed wire. Most of the resistance was from newly dug in positions in front of and around the pillboxes. Before we left Ancerville we found some schnapps and several men, including Chaney who was now a squad leader, drank a good bit and acquired a good dose of artificial courage. We moved up to the departure point and shed our overcoats and overshoes for the sake of mobility. The attack moved across an open field, where we received some light small arms fire, and into a rather open hardwood forest. The Third Platoon, which the mortar section was following, became separated from the rest of the company and we moved in the general direction we knew the attack was to follow.

Chaney, who was pretty high on schnapps, was moving well ahead of the mortar section. He was acting as section leader; I was trying to keep in touch with him and keep the rest of the section in touch with me. As the two of us would move through the woods a German or, occasionally a group of two or three Germans, would jump up and run away from us through the forest. We would try to get a shot at them as they ducked around the trees attempting to escape. It reminded me of shooting quail in the woods, snap shots with only a glimpse of the target. On one occasion three or four of them suddenly stood up out of a foxhole not ten feet in front of us, put their hands over head and yelled "Kamerad", the word for surrender in the European war. We would just motion them on back to the rest of the section after one of us checked them for weapons.

After we had moved for some distance we encountered a belt of pine trees and some barbed wire. By that time Sgt. Pierce had found us and let us know in no uncertain terms that he did not like the section's rather sloppy way of attacking solo. There were concrete bunkers in front of us which offered some resistance. We had a section of combat engineers with the company and they attacked the bunker with flame throwers. These consisted of a tank of fuel, carried on the back of the man with the flame thrower, with an attached hose and nozzle. The flame thrower sent out a jet of fire and very heavy black smoke thirty or forty feet and was directed at the embrasures or firing slots in the bunker. The fuel was thick and viscous and burned for some little while after it was fired. It took only one or two squirts of the fuel to produce a white flag and cries of "Kamerad" were heard as several very sooty looking Germans emerged from the bunker. Several bunkers were "buttoned up," that is the embrasures were closed with metal plates and not amenable to effective flame thrower attack. The engineers used satchel or pole charges on these, placing an explosive charge against the obstructing metal plates and blowing the plates in. The embrasures were kept under constant small arms fire to keep them buttoned up until the charge was placed but it took a lot of courage to run up to the bunker, laden with TNT, and place the charge against the port. The explosion usually resulted in mass exodus from the bunker, usually with a lot of men with ruptured ear drums.

This group of bunkers, none very large, constituted Fort Sorby which was one of the minor forts surrounding Metz. We cleared them with few casualties but did have some excitement when we heard several tanks on the edge of the woods while we were attacking the bunkers. We initially thought they were German tanks and were concerned because we had no known armor in support of us. Infantry without antitank weapons is quite vulnerable and it is frightening to be under attack by armor with no defense. However, the tanks turned out to be our 735th Tankers. In fact we dug in that night, in the rain as usual, in the laager of the tanks. The laager was a defensive position they took, facing peripherally, with infantry dug in around them.

The next day we moved out of the woods to attack across an open field. Just before we emerged from the woods the mortar section passed by one of the rifle platoons. Sgt. Hefner, an old platoon sergeant who had the unusual habit of carrying a large alarm clock in his jacket pocket, was lying face down. We thought he was dead as there had been some shelling and small arms fire in the area. However, he was just asleep. It may seem surprising but it was not unusual for men to go to sleep on the battlefield in spite of all the noise and danger. We moved out of the woods with supporting overhead machine gun fire and light tank support, across an open field, across railroad tracks and up a hill under some enemy 88 mm. fire to enter the small town of Ar-Laquenexy where we spent the night. On November 19th we made contact with the 90th Infantry Division at Puche, sealing the encirclement of Metz.

The city was visible to the naked eye, at last.

November 23. I'm getting along as well as can be expected. There's no use in my painting a rosy picture of the life we lead over here. It's rough, there's no doubt about it, but I've been at it for four months and I see no reason why I can't go to the end of it. The cut under my eye is just about healed and probably won't even leave a scar.

I'm always glad to get pictures from home even though they do make me homesick. The way I rate the hardships over here is: 1. being out in the weather all the time, 2. being away from home and 3. being shot at. Not that I like being shot at but if you get it you're either dead and don't have any more of this or you're wounded and in a hospital.

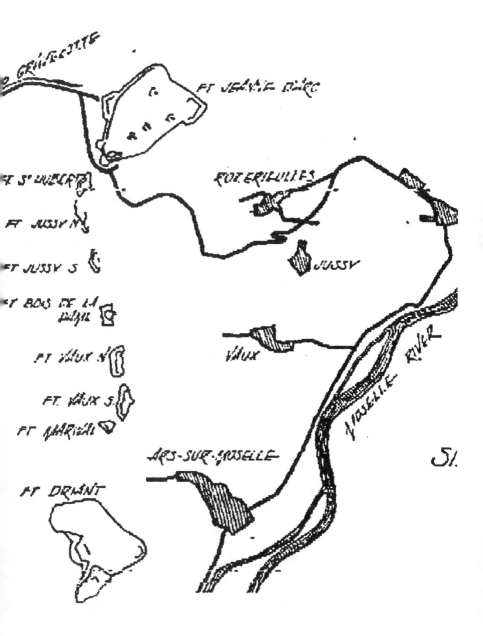

109

Main blockhouse of Fort Driant, shown after the fort surrendered.

Easy Living

We were billeted in barns and houses in a small village for a few days and, while we had to pull some guard duty, life was rather tranquil. Hot meals were resumed and I even got a can of squirrel, killed in Morgan County, Kentucky, which I relished. We watched artillery units firing missions and continued to take prisoners, either on foot or in vehicles, as they became aware of the fact that they were cut off and had little alternative in spite of the fact that Hitler had ordered them to hold out to the bitter end. Most of the troops surrendering were noncombatant rear echelon people. The diehards were holding out in the major forts on the west bank of the Moselle and continued to cause some trouble with occasional shelling and probing patrols, hoping to find a way out of Metz.

Metz was officially captured on November 21st though Forts Jean de Arc, Driant and the "Seven Dwarfs" ,which were minor forts between the two, still held out. The city was officially turned over to the French on the 24th. Two soldiers from each rifle company in the 5th and 95th Divisions were selected to be in an honor guard at the ceremony of transfer of control. Chaney and I were selected from Able Company. We were driven into the square next to the cathedral and assumed formation in the square. We had a chance to recover overcoats from our bed rolls but overall we were pretty raunchy looking troops, still wearing the mud covered boots and rather dirty uniforms that I, for one, had worn when I slept in mud and manure on the floor of a barn in Louvigny. We did have divisional patches on our uniforms and a red diamond on our helmets but some of the helmets had camouflage netting and some did not. We were, after all, combat troops and not garrison soldiers. Good looks was not in our job description. Our weapons were beaten up a bit but clean and functional.

As I recall, the day was overcast and chilly. We stood at ease while some of the dignitaries arrived. Then we heard the French troops coming into the square, heralded by a military band playing that rapid 140-beat-a-minute French military cadence. (Ours was 120) Their troops were spotless: olive drab pants and short jackets, black berets, spotless white leggings and Sam Browne belts, each with a sling over each shoulder supporting a submachine gun under each arm. Two submachine guns! The contrast between their impeccable appearance and ours was probably striking. They were heralded into the square with a fanfare, colors flying while we quietly marched in, though probably at attention for the first time in four months. They were garrison soldiers, we liberated the city. Aside from providing some information, rather late in the game for which they are not to blame, the French had little to do with the liberation of Lorraine but the French First Army was active further south in Alsace.

When I later had a pass to Paris I felt more of a sense of comradeship with some French front line troops on furlough from the fighting in Alsace, with whom I had some very garbled mixed language conversations about the war, than I did with the American garrison troops stationed around Paris.

General Walker, the Corps commander, took part in the ceremony, turning the city back to the French. The Star Spangled Banner and the Marseillaise were played and we presented arms with each. I still feel a thrill when I hear either and I still feel that I own at least a little of France.

After the ceremony A Company was loaded up in trucks and we returned to the hills on the west bank to contain the forts that still held out. The hills to the west of Metz are steep and high; the forts have a commanding view of the surrounding terrain. We went into Fort Deguise, one of the large forts which had been abandoned . It was a concrete fort at least three stories deep, surrounded by steel picket type fences about ten feet high, barbed wire and a dry concrete moat. It had a self contained electrical and water system but both were booby trapped and we depended for light on gasoline filled canteens with sock wicks which produced a maximum amount of smoke and a minimum of light. We all coughed and spit black carbon sputum for a month after we left. I wonder if anyone got black lung disease. The cooking area and company headquarters had Coleman type lanterns. We had hot food and a dry concrete floor to sleep on. We kept a close eye on the area of the surrounding forts though we could not see them directly, sent probing patrols to the area of the enemy occupied positions and fired a few harassing rounds of mortar fire, the latter primarily to bring our recent replacements up to par.

On the morning of December 8th Fort Driant, the last to hold out, surrendered. We were relieved that day by the 87th Infantry Division and left the Metz sector for the last time. It was not soon enough. The war was far from over and there was lots of mud and fighting to face but nothing began to equal the Metz campaign- the battle that should never have been.

We moved by truck to the coalmining town of Creutzwald, just west of the prewar Franco-German border, preparatory to attacking the Siegfried line of fortifications on the east bank of the Saar River, the prewar border of Germany. We were billeted in homes and practiced assault tactics against Maginot line fortifications on the east bank of the river for eight days. It seemed rather odd that mining operations were continuing without apparent interruption in spite of the war.

December 3rd-It is strange that there are reports of my divison's actions in the paper and I can make no comment about it but you know as much as I do about it. This is the best fighting outfit there is even if we do have to spear head the drives. In case you don't know it, this is Patton's first team.

Well, my Christmas packages have begun to roll in, one from you and Betty Jean and two from Mom and Dad. My demolition team will get to work and we'll take care of them in the prescribed manner.

I understand xxx (the son of a local politician) got a discharge even though he's in good physical condition, some people just pull strings and let others do the fighting for them. After you see your friends get killed it ceases to be something that can easily be put aside. There are very few men who do the fighting in this war and I know that every doggie and tanker is as sick of it as I am. And I'm sick of labor striking for more pay and shorter hours when we're out of shells because of their strike. It made me mad to read about Elsa Maxwell, the Washington socialite, throwing a big party to celebrate the liberation of France.

Chaney is sitting here next to me and he says the same thing goes for him. I'm mad and he's madder. He's been over here three years, never had a furlough and is beginning to feel that people in the States don't care how long he stays. A lot of boys in this outfit feel the same way.

Don't mind me, I'm just blowing my top. I'll go to the end of this, I'd still rather live in the States than anywhere else in the world and I'll fight for it. Maybe they (the censor) won't pass this, if they don't I can burn it. I promise I won't put any more ideas like this in print. Don't think I'm growling at you all, I know you're 100% behind us.

We few, we happy few, we band of brothers:
For he today that sheds his blood with me
Shall be my brother: be he ne'err so vile,
This day shall gentle his condition.
And every gentleman in England, now abed,
Shall think themselves accursed they were not here;
And hold their manhoods cheap whiles any speaks
That fought with us on St. Crispin's day.
Henry V, *Shakespeare*

A Short Violent Tour of the Reich

Hang Your Clothes on the Siegfried Line
Line from a song of the Second World War

On December 17th we entered Germany, crossing the Saar on a bridge captured by the 95th Division and relieving the 95th, who had been fighting in the cities of Saarlautern and Kaiserslautern, both now constituting the town of Saarlouis. The relief was carried out in daytime, the only occasion I can recall that we made a daytime relief. We walked into the area under constant air cover, P-47s were strafing and bombing enemy positions on the east bank of the river. The day was overcast and rather dark. Fighting on the approaches to the city had obviously been heavy and violent as the buildings along the road had been destroyed and there were a number of knocked out tanks, both American and German. Debris was scattered all along the road and it's environs. The impression I had was that everything was muddy and black with charred remains of buildings and vehicles. A few dead German soldiers were scattered along the roadside to complete the cheerful scene. As we approached the river we began to pass through areas of intermittent heavy shell fire. We passed a number of 95th Division troops standing around a jeep on the east bank, among them my nephew, W.P. Mayhew, an officer in the Battalion Headquarters of the unit we relieved though I did not recognize him at the time. We both could clearly recall the time and place after the war.

The mortar section moved into the wine cellar of a badly battered theatre. This initially seemed to be an excellent location as the cellar had a thick concrete roof and was as safe as could be under the circumstance. However, someone wanted some wine and knocked the bung out of a huge wine barrel, flooding the cellar ankle deep in white wine. We had to try to sleep lying on huge wine barrels, quite a feat. Luckily, they were immediately adjacent to one another and one could sleep, uncomfortably to be sure, in the trough between them. We set up the guns next to a pillbox adjacent to the theatre. During the time we were there an average of 2500 shells a day fell in the rather small area of the city we occupied. The enemy apparently had excellent observation from tall slag piles in the area. Whenever we fired a 60 mm. mortar mission we got immediate counter battery fire on our position but luckily had no casualties in the section.

The town was heavily fortified with pillboxes at every vantage point, cleverly camouflaged as shops, coal piles, homes etc. This was street fighting at it's worst. The use of the streets was denied by machine gun and 20 mm. fire and movement from one house to the next was usually through holes blasted in adjoining walls. In four days we cleared 232 buildings and 5 pill boxes, finally reaching the edge of the town. A Ranger battalion next to us moved a bit more rapidly, as might have been expected, they were elite troops.

We had quite a few casualties in the rifle platoons. One of my friends was sleeping in the basement of a house when he was awakened by a loud noise to find that an artillery shell had come through the wall of the building, landing a couple of feet from him but it failed to explode. He had a bad case of combat fatigue, called shell shock in World War One, and had to be evacuated and never returned to the company.

The battalion headquarters company usually did not have casualty rates as high as those in the rifle companies but in Saarlautern the communications section of the company had a very high casualty rate as a result of the continuous shelling. Communication with the various companies was usually by means of telephone wire, laid with hand carried spools and extended from Headquarters Company to the various rifle and weapons companies. The shelling constantly destroyed the wires and it was not unusual for wire in the process of being laid as replacement wire to be destroyed, with the men laying the wire becoming casualties as well. As a result ,we had to rely to a greater extent than usual on radio which was not too reliable.

On the night of December 20th we were told that we were to be relieved by the 95th Division. We had a number of dead in the area and were told that the Graves Registration Office personnel, who normally removed the dead after we pushed on, would not come up to evacuate them in this situation, where every movement was hotly contested. That night we took stretchers and tried, as best we could, to evacuate the dead as the plan was to fall back and consolidate the bridgehead across the Saar into a smaller area. The 5th Division was to go north and attack the southern flank of the German penetration into Luxembourg and Belgium as part of what became known as the Battle of the Bulge. Most of the dead were in buildings and had to be felt for rather than seen. Occasionally first discovery of a body came when the searcher's hand encountered the interior of an exposed brain or abdominal cavity, unpleasant to say the least. We had a few casualties while evacuating the dead which was bitterly resented but was understandable since there was no idea of when the offense in the area would resume and we did not want to leave the dead in enemy hands to become classed as permanently missing in action.

The night of the 21st we were relieved, under enemy fire, by the 377th

Infantry of the 95th Division, the same unit we had earlier relieved in Sauerlautern. I was not unhappy to leave that gloomy destroyed wreck of an industrial city with its shattered factories and its constant shell fire. There was a song written during the war that had a line about hanging your clothes on the Siegfried Line. It was not a popular song among the men who fought there.

Two of the members of the platoon, one a sergeant and the other a Pfc. runner, decided that they had had enough of infantry combat. They slipped away and somehow made their way to Paris where they became involved in the flourishing black market dealing with American military supplies. The Pfc. stayed a few days but his conscience bothered him and he turned himself over to the military police, helping them break up at least one black market ring. He returned to the company and served honorably until he was killed at the subsequent Mosel crossing. The sergeant was caught and court martialed.

The trip north to the Ardennes was made largely at night. We moved during a snowstorm at a very slow pace with full headlights on, very unusual as vehicle movements at night usually had only "cat's eyes" which were small blue lights on front and back of the vehicle to prevent collisions. They were only visible a few feet from the light. Had we traveled with only "cat's eyes" we would have been hours longer in arriving in Luxembourg. The situation there demanded immediate reinforcements and it was deemed that the risk of being hit by enemy night fighters or bombers was low so we went fully lit. We could hear a good bit of aerial activity over us but assumed that we were hearing our "Black Widow" night fighters and had no enemy interference. It was bitterly cold in open trucks. Under combat conditions we never put the canvas tops over the truck beds for shelter. When we had to leave under fire we wanted out: over the sides, the back, any way. The trip was uneventful except for occasional vehicles having minor accidents.

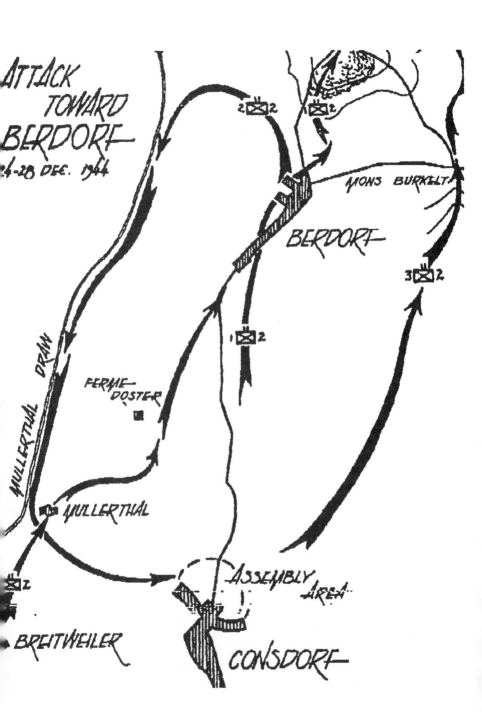

ATTACK
TOWARD
BERDORF
24-28 DEC. 1944

2 ⊠ 2

2 ⊠ 2

MONS BURKELT

BERDORF

3 ⊠ 2

1 ⊠ 2

MULLERTHAL DRAW

FERME
DOSTER

MULLERTHAL

ASSEMBLY
AREA

⊠ 2

BREITWEILER

CONSDORF

119

The Ardennes

We moved through the city of Luxembourg, mounted in trucks, on December 23rd. The countryside that day was covered with eight or ten inches of snow and the city, situated on hills bordered by vertical cliffs with deep ravines separating them , was spectacularly beautiful. It has been called the "Gibraltar of the North" and had the reputation of being impregnable. There was a great deal of military traffic in the area, German troops were not much more than 20 kilometers away and the American line was thinly held by the 12th Infantry Regiment of the 4th Infantry Division. We were billeted that night in a barn, fifty of us slept in the loft and slept very warmly, I might add, burrowed down into the hay. It was a bit prickly and hay tended to work its way down inside clothing but it was delightfully warm after the long cold truck ride. A barn full of hay was the dogface soldier's perfect place to sleep, unfortunately they were all too rare.

On Christmas Eve we moved up to Consdorf and spent the night, preparing to attack Burdorf, the next town to the north. We were billeted in a large stone barn filled with wonderful soft hay and were served a hot Christmas dinner. That evening the stars and moon were out in full glory. An artillery unit was quartered in the village and was well supplied with alcohol. They were singing the usual Christmas carols and it was quite pleasant to hear them singing in that Christmas-card-like snow covered village. The evening was marred only by occasional firing missions by the 155mm. "Long Tom" rifles. Unfortunately they fired directly over the barn we were in and the muzzle blast was terrific. There was a concrete "two holer" privy behind the barn we slept in. The area beneath the seat was open in the direction of the artillery pieces, thirty yards or so behind the privy. They were directed toward the privy although elevated to point above it. It was quite cold in the privy, not conducive to meditation but as I was seated there, doing what needed to be done, the big guns fired a mission and the concussion of the muzzle blast, coming in from below, produced a wave of frigid air that lifted me off of the seat. I did not linger!

Patton sent us a Christmas message and prayer as follows-

To each officer and soldier in the Third United States Army I wish a Merry Christmas. I have full confidence in your courage, dedication duty, and skill in battle. We march in our might to complete victory. May God's blessing rest upon each of you this Christmas Day.

G.S.Patton, Jr.
Lieutenant General
Third United States Army

This was on a small wallet sized card with the following prayer on the reverse side.

Prayer

Almighty and most merciful heavenly Father, we humbly beseech Thee, of thy great goodness to restrain these immoderate rains with which we have to contend. Grant us fair weather for Battle. Graciously hearken to us as soldiers who call upon Thee that armed with Thy power we may advance from victory to victory and crush the opposition and wickedness of our enemies and establish Thy justice among men and nations. Amen.

Believe it or not, the rain and snow ceased and the skies cleared. The chaplain should have gotten a promotion.

On Christmas day we prepared to attack but the attack was postponed, allowing us to attend church services. The Protestant church had been hit by artillery fire, knocking a hole in the roof and filling it with debris, but the interior was still usable and we filed in carrying our weapons, sang a few hymns and had a brief sermon though I don't recall it's content. All in all, the circumstances were not in keeping with the usual idea of peace on earth to men of good will.

In the darkness of late night or early morning we moved out to attack to the north, passing by many dead American 4th Division soldiers alongside a road that ran though a forested area. They were all facing to the north in the direction the enemy had come from, brave men who had held the German penetration. We swung toward the west along the east bank of the Mullerthal Draw, a deep wooded ravine. There was little small arms fire directed toward us but we received ample artillery fire, most of it bursting in the trees overhead and there were quite a few casualties from it. The fire moved forward as we did; we were obviously under direct observation in the woods but we could never spot who was directing it. The ravine was so deep that we could not cross it but suspected that the observer was on the opposite bank. Progress was slow, the attack continued into the early night but we took the high ground to the north of Berdorf.

This latter part of this attack was carried out using "artificial moonlight" created by searchlights shining on clouds, which dispersed or reflected the light so that we could see fairly well at night. We had none of the infrared scopes used by our armed forces in later military operations. The next day we moved into Berdorf, a small town which had seen some heavy fighting . The mortar section occupied the Parc Hotel, a small resort hotel on the north edge of the town. In one of the rooms on the second floor American .30 caliber machine gun casings were almost ankle deep and there were numerous German dead in a field just across the road.

Except for moderate enemy artillery fire, our stay in Berdorf was uneventful. We were relieved by the 12th Infantry Regiment, Fourth Infantry Division, on the 28th and went into reserve in Schieren, just south of the Sure River.

December 31st-Right now I have no complaints. I'm in a building with a stove and electric lights. Not bad, eh? This country is the most beautiful I've seen in Europe. Hilly and wooded, it reminds me of home. There's a light snow on the ground, has been for a while, and it looks like the picture you see of small towns in Europe in the winter. I prefer the hills of Kentucky a 1000 to 1. I spent a pretty good Christmas eve, slept in a hay loft and got several packages. It was a beautiful clear moonlit night and I didn't mind pulling guard duty. The days before and after were no picnic but as long as I can get a few good days like this I don't mind. In a way I don't like going from K and C rations to good solid regular chow. It always messes up my stomach for a few days.

Years later my wife and I went back to Burdorf and stayed at the Parc Hotel, now in a beautiful setting. The proprietor's wife was at the desk. I asked if she could speak English and she said "Yes, I am English." She had been there during the war and remembered events clearly.

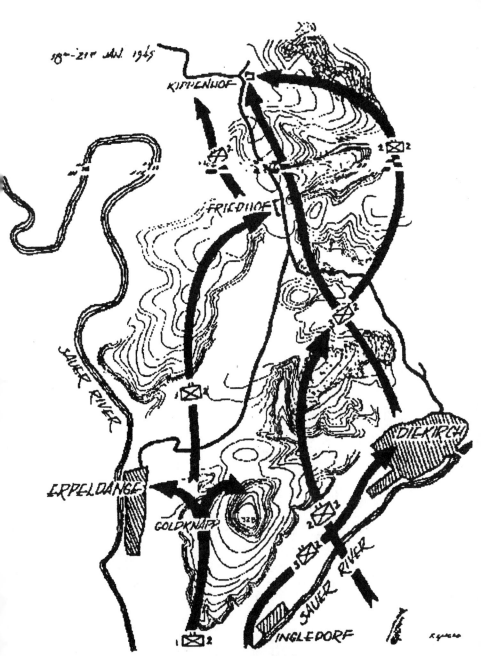

Diekirch area near site of German attack on the hill south of Friedhof after the Sure, also spelled Sauer, River crossing.

The First Sure River Crossing

By my troth, I care not: a man can die but once;
We owe God a death....And let it go which way it will.
He that dies this year is quit for the next.
Shakespeare.

On the way to Schieren we marched through some rather dense forest and came to a crossroad which was being shelled intensely. A shell would hit in the immediate vicinity of the crossroad every minute or so and occasionally one would hit in random pattern in the surrounding woods so that there seemed to be no safe way to get by the crossroad, which we had to do. There were several wounded and dead men on or alongside the road as we approached. We spread the interval between men to twenty or thirty yards and tried to time a dash through the area so that we hoped to miss the fairly regularly timed incoming shells. Lt. Murphy, our company executive officer, who had spent a great deal of his combat time as acting company commander and who was highly regarded by everyone, was wounded by shrapnel at the crossroad. The wound was apparently in a lower extremity as he was unable to walk and he was expressing his opinion of Germans in no uncertain terms as I ran by him. I understand he was evacuated successfully but his wound was severe enough that he never came back up to the company.

For two weeks we alternated between being billeted in the small village of Schieren and being on the front situated on a hill overlooking the Sure River and the small enemy held towns of Erpeldange and Ettelbruck. While on the front we fired a few registering rounds on possible enemy positions but generally we just sat in foxholes in the snow covered ground and tried to keep warm. On one fire mission my gun had a misfire; the guiding vanes on the bottom of the shell broke off as the round fired and the shell tumbled after it emerged from the mortar and fell only a few feet in front of the gun. We knew it was a misfire, called for everyone to hit the dirt and no one was injured by the nearby explosion.

I might add a word here about the operation of a 60 mm. mortar. It consisted of a short nonrifled tube which had a fixed firing pin in the base. The mortar was fired by dropping the shell, after removing a safety pin which prevented detonation if not removed, into the tube. The shell had a firing charge, consisting of a shotgun shell on it's base and four separate charges of a green leaf-like explosive which were attached to the guiding vanes on it's base. It

"K Comp'ny artillery commander speakin'."
The worst thing about mortars is that the Germans make them too.

struck the firing pin, detonating the explosive charges, propelling the shell in a high arching trajectory to it's target. The "business end" of the shell consisted of an explosive charge detonating when the shell struck, scattering shrapnel. The complete shell weighed about three pounds. The firing range of the mortar was two thousand yards and was varied by adjusting the angle of elevation by an elevating screw on a two legged support, called a bipod, attached to the tube and by varying the number of "increments," which we called the leaf-like attached charges. Initial firing direction was given by compass bearing and then adjusted by a traversing scale, graduated in mils. Usually several "zeroing in" rounds were fired until one of the guns was on target, then all three guns fired three rounds or more "for effect". I have read that mortars caused more casualties than any other weapon in The Second World War.

Bill Mauldin comments in his book *Up Front* that "Mortars are the artillery of an infantry company. Outside of the bazooka, they carry more viciousness and wallop per pound than any other weapon the infantry has. The guys who operate them are at a big disadvantage because of the mortars limited range. They have to work so close to the front they are a favorite target for snipers, patrols, shells and counter mortar fire. Knocked out mortar positions earn Iron Crosses for ambitious Herrenvolk."

One night the company commander, a platoon leader and a sergeant were checking the outpost line situated near the river. This was manned only at night to give warning that an enemy patrol or attack was crossing the river under cover of darkness. A replacement soldier with only a few days combat experience was on the outpost line. The group checking the outpost missed him in the dark, went beyond him to the river's edge and then approached the outpost from the direction of the river. The replacement thought they were an enemy patrol, did not halt them or call for the password and killed the company commander.

When we were in the houses in the village, after a few days at the front, we made occasional patrols along the river bank and around a collapsed bridge over the river in the town of Ettelbruck, a small town largely on the north side of the river. On one night one of the riflemen named Booth, who was from New Orleans and had a great sense of humor, was killed by machine gun fire while trying to crawl across the river on the bridge. It is ironic that the river is quite shallow and could easily be waded in most areas without being in water more than knee deep.

One evening we had word from a prisoner that a German combat patrol was expected to cross the river in front of us and several men from the weapons platoon and one of the rifle platoons formed a combat patrol to deal with the expected enemy attack. A combat patrol consisted of a fairly large group and expected to fight, in fact was to look for a fight, in contrast to a reconnaissance patrol which usually consisted of four or five men and usually avoided any combat. We spent most of the night lying in the snow, scattered up and down the river bank, but Jerry did not appear. After it was obvious that no enemy would appear that night we made our way up the hill to the battalion headquarters which was in a large building on the forward slope of the hill. As we walked around the corner of the building a new replacement on guard failed to challenge us and shot and killed the sergeant leading the patrol. Such accidents were not rare. An old platoon sergeant, Joe Neff, completed his thirty years in service and was sent back to the Verdun area for transfer to the States but was accidentally shot and killed by a replacement in a replacement center who was preparing to clean his rifle.

My wife and I visited Ettelbruck in the 1980s. There is a statue of Patton in a park on the edge of town. He stands with field glasses in his hand, looking at the building where we returned from the patrol and the patrol leader died from our own "friendly"fire.

On the night of January 17th the temperature dropped to 16 degrees Fahrenheit and there was twelve inches of new snow. We made an attack across the Sure River which was only about forty feet wide and rarely over waist deep in that area. The engineers had laid a foot bridge, a simple floating bridge about three feet wide floating on small pontoons, across the river. As my platoon moved onto the bridge one of the ammo bearers in my squad refused to go any further. I was the gunner at the time and was carrying the mortar. It seemed rather foolish to me to carry the mortar with only two ammo bearers and only 36 rounds of ammunition so I took the extra packboard from the man who refused to carry on and started to cross the river. The rest of the platoon had moved on a hundred feet or so and the bridge had broken while I was arguing with him so I had to wade the knee deep river. The engineers had laid fluorescent tapes through the cleared area of the mine field on the enemy side of the river. I was too tired and mad to follow the tape which meandered a bit so I took a short cut directly through the uncleared area to the men in my platoon. The mines, as well as the ground, may have been frozen which may account for the fact that I failed to detonate any. We had moderately heavy resistance as we took the little village of Erpeldange and moved on to the Goldknapp Hill beyond it.

As we moved along the high ground to the north in the fog and snow and as daylight came, we noted several tanks and infantrymen in white uniforms in a valley several hundred yards to our left. No American troops were supposed to be there and we opened fire on them. I don't know what effect our fire had on them but we were quickly informed that they were men of the 80th Infantry Division. Since they had on white camouflage, as did we, such mistakes were inevitable. Somewhat later that day we began to receive accurate heavy artillery fire. The company had halted along the roadside and I looked around for shelter from the shelling. There was a culvert under the road and I crawled into it, crawling to the end to let others in behind me. Iron bars covered the far end of the culvert and I became claustrophobic, thinking that someone behind me would be killed and I would not be able to get out. That didn't last long as the company moved out very soon.

As darkness fell on that short, cloudy, snowy day we moved into some mixed hardwood and pine forest and set up for the night. The ground was frozen, we had met only light resistance and we scrapped out very shallow foxholes. Andy and I dug in together and we couldn't have dug deeper than five or six inches. In the late night one of the men in the platoon, who had a reputation of being a bit more nervous than many others, woke Lt. Dahlrymple to tell him that he had seen some German troops moving across a field toward the woods we were occupying at the time. The lieutenant looked for a minute or two, told him he had just seen some sheep, that there was nothing to worry about, and went back to sleep.

Ten or fifteen minutes later all hell broke loose! The Germans, in white, had slipped to within forty or fifty feet of us and caught us in shallow holes, totally unprepared for them. I was in a mummy like sleeping bag, face down. I knew what was going on-there was "burp gun" German submachine gun fire only a few feet from me and I thought I would never find the zipper on the bag and get out of it. There was a narrow band of small pine trees between Andy and me and the Germans. Captain Jones and Sgt. Stein, the first sergeant, were sleeping in the pines. The captain personally killed 11 Germans with his pistol for which he received the Distinguished Service Cross, well deserved. Sgt. Stein was killed and a number of men were bayoneted in their sleeping bags. I never slept in one again. I came out of the bag barefooted, having taken my wet shoes off before getting in.. We formed up a hundred feet or so from the pine trees and then cleared the enemy position. I think Captain Jones actually accounted for the majority of the enemy casualties. He was an excellent company commander but I think he would have preferred being in a paratroop unit; he had been a paratrooper but was not sent back to the paratroops after he was wounded in Italy.

We continued to attack along the ridge to the north, moving through woods and pasture land with light resistance, until we received moderate small arms fire from the vicinity of a farmhouse slightly below the crest of the ridge. We spread the company out on a broad front and moved forward with every one firing away, so called" marching fire." In this case it worked quite well as the opposition was rather light. Normally, the riflemen would hit the dirt and then advance by short rushes before going to ground again, the men on the ground giving covering fire as others advanced in leapfrog manner. Most of the German opposition here was killed as I recall very few prisoners. A short while later we caught some incoming artillery fire and I pulled a young dead German soldier who had been shot in the forehead from his foxhole to use it myself. It was a somewhat uncomfortable feeling but I was glad to have the hole there.

The proximity artillery fuse was used in combat for the first time during the Ardennes campaign. Artillery fire is most effective against infantry if the shell explodes a few feet above the ground. The shrapnel from such an explosion spreads in a ball shaped manner and is even effective against men in uncovered foxholes. The fuse of a shell could be timed to explode near impact but the timing was critical and not always accurate. A shell striking the ground threw shrapnel in an inverted cone shape and "hitting the dirt" gave a fair degree of protection and a foxhole or slit trench gave protection against anything but a direct hit. The proximity fuse apparently had a sort of radar device in it and exploded at any desired distance above the ground. It was very effective but had one unintended bad effect. If the shell passed over friendly troops on high ground before descending to strike the enemy on lower ground it occasionally exploded over the friendly troops. We had several casualties from this effect until the problem was recognized.

On January 28th we relieved the 10th and 11th Infantry on a static line overlooking the Our river, a tributary of the Sure River, west Of Vianden. There was little combat activity but the weather was bitterly cold and we had quite a few men who developed trench foot or frostbite. Shortly thereafter we were relieved and had a few days of training preparing to assault the Siegfried line on the eastern, and therefore German, side of the Sure River. During this time we were billeted in a school house and had a chance to be warm and dry for a change.

My brother Harold sent me a pair of combat boots which were quite welcome. They were easier to put on than the legging and shoe combination we had been wearing and they looked a bit sharper and neater. They were supposed to be sent to the infantry but the rear echelon troops in the quartermaster corps "short stopped" them and we got them quite late. PBI-"Poor Bloody Infantry." Harold was a captain and officers in combat units could buy boots, which is how he got them to me. We had been issued shoe pacs, much like L.L. Bean's famous shoe pacs. They did keep our feet drier than GI shoes but were not as supportive on long marches and the combat boots were more comfortable. Our feet were constantly wet, we were issued socks on a frequent basis but they were wet within a few minutes after changing them. There was a directive that a soldier who developed trench foot could be court martialed but I don't think it was ever pursued. There weren't enough officers to meet the demand.

I might make comment here about some problems of all infantrymen in a cold, damp climate. If you dress warmly enough to be comfortable when you are not moving you sweat when you are active. Then when you stop the moisture of the sweat makes the cold that much worse. Overcoats were issued but were entirely unsatisfactory for troops on the move. You carry too much equipment to fight with to permit carrying extra clothing when you stop. Green troops always carry too much. That may be one reason they have a relatively high casualty rate compared to seasoned troops. Weight slows you down when you need speed. Go as lightly as you can.

Another big problem was getting supplies up to the men at the front.

Supplies had to come in at night and usually had to be hand carried. Vehicles made too much noise and drew artillery fire. The German Army kitchens were horse drawn and came up as close to the front as they could at night, sometimes giving us an audible clue regarding their positions. Their field rations were far inferior to ours, probably the one area we were superior in regard to field equipment. They usually just had some black bread, an onion or two and some precooked sausage. We were usually dug in some distance from the nearest road unless we defended a village. Carrying a pack board of mortar or machine gun ammunition up a steep, muddy hill on a rainy night when you can't see three feet in front of you, falling and sliding back two feet for every three in a forward direction quickly rids one of the notion of the glory of war. Fighting by day and being in a carrying party at night creates an attitude of pacifism..

January 14th- I'm enjoying life at present. I'm in a rest camp and could stay here for the duration, slept in a bed last night for the first time since entering France. Plenty of good chow, even had pie for supper and there's a movie every night. As further evidence of luxury I even had a bath in a bathtub this morning. The only catch is I'm only here for two days. I read that Sgt. Kelly (a Congressional Medal winner) said that the greatest thrill in the world is to risk your life and come out alive, it fills your veins with soda pop bubbles. He's right, it's a big thrill, not the part about risking your life but the part about coming out alive.

It's a funny world; here we are over here cutting down the world's population every day and back home they're having more babies than ever. Next thing you know we'll be pushing for lebensraum.

February 5th- We're back in the mud again, the snow has thawed and it rains instead of snowing, It's not as cold but I'd just as soon have snow instead of this mud. The Russians seem to be doing well, hope they can keep it up.

Germany Again

O Polly love, O Polly love, the rout has now begun,
And we must be a-marching at the beating of the drum;
Go dress yourself in all your best and come along with me,
I'll take you to the cruel war in high Germany.

High Germany-Anonymous

While the 2nd Infantry was in dry quarters for a few days the 10th and 11th Infantry were making a river crossing across the Sauer River, which was in flood following the thawing of the snow. It was a difficult crossing, complicated by barbed wire concealed by the flood waters so that the assault boats hung up on the wire and the assault troops had to disembark into the barbed wire. The river ran through a deep valley and numerous pill boxes on the east side of the river commanded the river bank to a deadly degree.

We relieved the 10th Infantry on the 15th of February near Bollendorf, a small town on the German bank of the river, and attacked through the hilly forest and the pillboxes of the Siegfried line toward the village of Shankweiler. There was intense artillery, Screaming Meemie and machine gun fire en route but by the 16th the village was in our hands and we pushed on to cross the Enz River and captured a bridge across the Prum River. These were small rivers in deep ravines traversing the hilly wooded country. The geographic area here is called the Eifel; it is an extension of the same type of terrain called the Ardennes in Belgium and Luxembourg. By this time we had pushed through the Siegfried line but there was still rather stiff resistance. Movement was hindered by heavy rainfall with the usual mud. The engineers had to fell trees and construct corduroy roads to make them usable for our support vehicles.

After we crossed the Prum near Stockem we moved up to the high ground on the east bank under rocket fire and dug in in the late afternoon in an open pine woods. The weapons platoon lost contact with much of the company in the late afternoon and we were late in getting into position and had no idea of where the other platoons were. Shortly after daylight the next morning a German officer and an enlisted man came strolling up a path in the woods, apparently totally unaware that we were there. I think we were as surprised as they were. The officer attempted to swing his Schmeisser machine pistol into firing position but he and his companion were cut down before they could fire on us.

Yours truly, taken in Paris, February 21st, 1945.
Looks reasonably sober and not unduly dissipated?

Shortly thereafter we began to take 88 mm. fire from two enemy tanks moving up the hill toward us, supported by a hundred or so infantry. We had a bazooka man (a bazooka was a tube like rocket launcher used as an antitank weapon) named Patey, from Richmond, Virginia, who was a very cool soldier. He left our lines and moved down the hill, in with the German infantry, who apparently were either blind or too astonished to shoot him, got in behind the Panther tank where it was most vulnerable, knocked it out with the bazooka, and casually made his way back to our lines unharmed. It was the most incredible incident I have ever seen. The other tank pulled back and our small arms fire broke up the enemy attack.

Later in the day we pushed on and dug in, again on a forested hilltop. I had time to dig a fairly deep hole and cover it with logs and a foot or so of dirt, topped off with my shelter half. I must have slept very soundly when not on the usual two hours on, two off watch as I woke the next morning to find my shelter half riddled with shrapnel from an artillery shell burst in a tree directly overhead. I never heard the shell strike.

That was about the end of my experience in the Ardennes campaign. It was, for me, aside from the winter weather, not as bitter as the fighting in the Metz area but we did not bear the brunt of the initial attack, which fell primarily on the 99th and 106th Divisions. The 106th was essentially wiped out and most of the infantry in the 99th, which was my brother Harold's unit, became casualties. My brother, who was in an artillery unit, narrowly escaped physical injury.

March 5th- The impossible can, and often does, happen. I got a three day pass to Paris, believe it or not. And I really had a good time, had a good bed with sheets , hot chow, entertainment and Coca Cola! The women really go in for perfume, you can smell a gal coming a block away.

Gay Paree

How are you going to keep them down on the farm
after they've seen Paree?
Vintage song from World War One

At this point I got a reprieve, a three day pass to Paris. The division had initiated a policy of sending one man at a time from each company for three days in Paris. By this time I was an old timer. The company had had over 1200 replacements, many killed and wounded, a few taken prisoner but some due to non battle injuries and combat fatigue. During the fall campaign when infantry casualty rates were so high we got replacements from quartermaster, ordinance and medical units who were not physically or psychologically fit for infantry combat. Some of them fell out on very short marches and just could not sustain the stress. There were few of the old timers left.

O'Conner, one of our mortar men, had just returned from Paris. He had a black eye and various cuts and bruises on his face and took a bit of kidding about those physical women in Paris. Some of the men returning were "Whores de combat" from brawls over women or venereal disease acquired there and he was accused of that. Nothing like sad facts to kill a good story. It turned out that he was in Bollendorf awaiting transportation to Paris and some "Long Tom" 155 mm. artillery pieces fired across the building he was in and the muzzle blast dislodged some plaster which fell on his face while he slept.

I went back to Bollendorf and spent the night, billeted in a room with plaster hanging from the ceiling, possibly O'Conner's nemesis. While I was there General Patton came through in an open jeep, complete with the red three star general's flag, polished helmet, ivory handled pistols and all. A very colorful man who, contrary to some reports from rear echelon types, was greatly respected by the combat troops in his command. His philosophy was to hit hard, bypass any opposition if possible, and keep rolling. Some called him "Old Blood and Guts, our blood and his guts", but we believed that his tactics, in contrast to Montgomery's slow, methodical tactics, got better results and shortened the war.

The next day I rode a truck to a point near Rheims, where we spent the night. On the following day we were taken to a Quartermaster depot in Paris, turned in our dirty torn uniforms and had a hot shower. I threw away two sets of long john underwear and a sweat suit I had not had off of my body since

139

December. We were issued new uniforms and taken to the Grand Hotel, not the famous one but a small hotel out of the exclusive hotel area in the city. I spent a fair amount of time in the bathtub, relaxing in the hot water which seemed heavenly. And clean soft sheets!

I enjoyed riding the Metro subway, which was clean and it was easy to find my way around in it. I went to a show in the Olympic Theatre and saw the Glenn Miller Orchestra, though he had been lost in a plane crossing the English Channel. One evening I went to the Folies Bergere and I went out to one of the parks and rode a camel in the zoo. The Champs Elysee and the Arc de Triumph were impressive. The bars closed about midnight; after that the only places serving drinks were the brothels. One of the men from B Company and I caught a bicycle propelled two seat pedicab and told the driver we wanted a drink. He took us to a rather elaborate cat house with a spiral staircase. There was a bar at the foot of the steps and women were lined up on the steps, take your pick of girls with green hair, blue hair etc., all piled on top of their heads, scantily clad in dim light. Most of them looked old enough to be my grandmother. My companion picked one out of the line and took her up to a room but came back down promptly when he saw her in a decent light. Business seemed to pretty brisk but we had seen enough and headed back to the Grand Hotel.

Our meals were GI rations but prepared by French chefs and accompanied by chamber music; a far cry from the meals at the front but it only lasted three days.

t Battalion, 2nd Infantry attack
om Oberkail

German Counterattack

OBERKAIL

SCHWARZENBORN

EISENSCHMITT

EICHELL

GRANSDORF

2nd Battalion attack

SCHWARZENBORN
—6-7· MARCH· 1945·

Back to the Front

The company was in a wooded area near the town of Bitburg, an important crossroad town between Aachen and Trier, which had been heavily bombed during the Ardennes campaign. It was as badly damaged as St. Lo; bulldozers had to push a route through the rubble filled streets. We made a crossing of the Nims, another small stream, and left Bitburg mounted in trucks. We were moving in association with the 4th Armored Division. Colonel Abrams, one of their combat commanders, made the famous statement, "It's Katy bar the door for the Rhine." The division moved in classic Third Army style, bypassing opposition and leaving it for us to clean up. They reached the Rhine within forty-eight hours. We paused to make a crossing of the Kyle River on March 6th and captured the village of Oberkail.

That night we moved on foot toward the village of Schwartzenborn. We had to pass through a shallow ravine, which was blocked by fallen trees, before we approached the town. As the lead elements of the company neared the village Jerry opened up with small arms and armored self propelled guns. Enemy troops were in the village and the surrounding woods in considerable number. The village itself consisted of only a few buildings, the largest on the near side of the town consisting of a typical bulky stone farmhouse and attached barn. We captured the barn and found that there were a number of German wounded and medics who had not been evacuated. A short while later a German tank pulled up to the barn, supported by heavy small arms fire, and fired into the barn with the muzzle of the gun protruding into the building. The muzzle blast was terrific, luckily they only got one round off before a bazooka man ran around behind the tank and fired a round at it. It did not knock the tank out but the tank crew realized how vulnerable they were in the dark and pulled back but continued to rake the area with shrapnel and machine gun fire.

The German infantry moved in closer, the situation was confused to say the least. Finally we called in friendly artillery fire on our own position and the enemy infantry pulled back enough for us to withdraw to the ravine west of town. We had to leave our wounded and some medics in the barn, mixed in with German medics and wounded men. There were heavy casualties-killed, wounded or captured. The next morning the 2nd Battalion moved through us and renewed the attack on Schwartzenborn but found that the enemy had pulled out. Our wounded and the German wounded were still in the barn.

As we moved forward to the east we found numerous signs painted on

stone walls or cliffs. "Many Roads Lead to the Rhine, Many More to Death," "See the Rhine and Leave Your Skull," "Die for Tommy" etc. There were a fair number of propaganda leaflets fired into our lines in artillery shells. We also fired them over to the Germans, usually in the form of a "Safe Conduct Pass" assuring them of good treatment. Most were used, both German and American, as toilet paper. The next two images are of one of theirs, front and back, rather

DEAD MEN TELL NO TALES NOR DO THEY KISS THEIR GIRLS

badly battered.

Another river crossing was made at Eisenschmitt, crossing the Salm Rver. We marched for twenty four hours encountering little resistance, which was usually quickly silenced by marching fire. In this area we found quite a few very young German soldiers, some probably no more than sixteen or seventeen. After a day or so of marching we mounted up in trucks and moved to the northeast, taking the towns of Daun, Ulmen, Masburg, and Biningen en route to Carden on the Mosel River. The Mosel (German spelling) is the downstream continuation of the Moselle (French spelling) in France.

Here we took up positions on the high ground overlooking the river. The winter weather had gone, the days were mild and the local countryside was pleasing to view. We billeted in houses, got clean clothes and hot meals again. Chaney even gave several of us haircuts. It all seemed rather unreal after the cold winter and bitter fighting of the past few months.

Here there were still many German civilians, until that time undisturbed directly by the war. Many were obviously and openly hostile to us, the younger women in particular. I'm sure many of them had lost husbands or boyfriends, killed or wounded, fighting Americans. There were also quite a few young men in civilian clothes with obvious residuals of combat wounds, amputations etc. They showed little evidence of hostility and seemed quite willing to converse with us.

Broken footbridge across the Mosel, medics and a wounded man on the bridge
I am the soldier wading the river.

The Second Mosel Crossing

The Mosel River runs through a wide gorge surrounded by hills that rise eight or nine hundred feet above the river which, in 1945, was about three or four hundred feet wide and was a moderately fast flowing stream. Since then a series of locks have raised the river, altering the waterfront. There were a number of old castles situated at strategic points on the high ground and the hillsides consisted largely of terraced vineyards, the source of the grapes for the noted Mosel wines.

After dark on the night of March 13th we moved down from the high ground on the north bank of the river into the town of Carden (also spelled Karden), which was situated on the river bank. The bank itself was cobblestoned down to and into the river, presumably to ease moving hogsheads of wine into river barges, which made it a bit easier to launch assault boats into the river. The "assault" boats were simply large pontoons which held about ten infantrymen and an engineer or two. They were about as graceful and easy to paddle as any box would be. Propulsion was by means of paddles initially, primarily to maintain silence and surprise as much as possible. When I read of assault boats "roaring" across rivers I have to laugh at the irony of the term. After a bridgehead was established the engineers used outboard motors to ferry the following waves of assault troops over the river and then used the same pontoons to construct floating pontoon bridges.

We assembled on the waterfront of the village, which was only about one house in depth and was strung out along the river, boxed in by the hill behind it. There were many wine cellars filled with large vats of wine but I don't recall anyone repeating our mistake of knocking out a bung and flooding a cellar as happened in Saarlautern. The pontoons were brought down to the waterfront by truck. We carried them down to the river and launched them for the assault, got in and paddled as quietly as possible across the river. There was a fairly brisk current and boats landed strung out along the far side of the river in the usual confused pattern of nocturnal river crossings. We took a little small arms fire; one boat was hit rather severely and drifted down the river with the haunting cries of the wounded for help fading away as the boat moved away from us in the darkness of the night. We could do nothing to help them. I have no idea what eventually happened to those men.

The south bank of the river was quite steep, a road ran alongside the river with a stone wall at the lower side of the terraced vineyard rising eight or nine feet above the road-a rather formidable obstacle for heavily burdened men in the weapons platoon. We scaled the wall and entered the vineyard to find a new similar wall facing us every hundred feet or so. Luckily, the vines and their supporting wires ran vertically up and down the hill so that they presented no obstacle. As we moved up the hill we began to receive small arms fire and numerous "potato masher" hand grenades rained down on us from Germans on the high ground ahead of us. Their grenades were shaped something like a potato masher, hence the name. They were lighter than ours but did not have the destructive effect that ours did as the removable shrapnel sleeve on their grenades threw lighter fragments than our "pineapple"grenades. However, there was in effect little soil to absorb the blast of the grenades. The vineyard soil was covered with pieces of flint up to three or four inches in size. I think the purpose was to retain heat but it also doubled the blast effect by throwing flint as well as shrapnel. Almost everyone was hit by some of the flint, usually with little effect if we were more than forty feet or so from the blast. There was a brisk exchange of grenades at distances of fifty to a hundred feet and we took several casualties from them. The hill seemed to be interminably high with one stone wall after another to scale. I think we outnumbered Jerry considerably or we never would have made it up the hill but we eventually broke out of the vineyard into some second growth forest near the top of the hill.

At that point the character of the fight changed to a predominately small arms affair. The mortar section tried to dig in on the edge of the woods. Chaney and Hank Terzago were digging about five or six feet from Andy and me. For some reason, at that time my hearing for the low pitched whisper of an incoming mortar round seemed to better than that of many others and I heard a round coming in and hit the dirt while the other three were still semi upright. I'm not sure that my position when the shell burst in the trees ten or fifteen feet above us made any difference but Hank was killed instantly by shrapnel which ripped open a long section of his spine, exposing and severing his spinal cord. Chaney suffered an abdominal wound and Andy was hit in the foot. Shanks was also wounded at about the same time. I didn't get a scratch.

We had no medic nearby and I violated the usual rule of combat by helping Andy and Chaney down to the foot of the hill. The usual procedure was for the infantry to keep fighting and let the medics take care of the wounded. It is said that it takes five men to care for one wounded eventually and, if all wounded were evacuated by fellow infantrymen, there would be no fighting men left on the average day of combat. At any rate I went to the foot of the hill and a medic and engineer asked me to help paddle a boatload of wounded across the river to the aid station in Karden which I did, this time not under fire.

I helped Andy to the aid station and then started back to the company. The engineers had thrown a footbridge across the river but it had been struck by shell fire and broken. The river between the shore and the bridge was shallow and I waded out to the bridge. Some medics had been carrying a litter with a wounded man on it when a shell broke the bridge and the wounded man had fallen into the river. Someone was holding him by the collar of his jacket as I came up to him but he was intermittently sinking beneath the surface of the water and the hold on him seemed precarious . He was very unhappy with the situation. I took my jacket off and jumped in, holding him up and in contact with the bridge until a pontoon boat with an outboard motor came up and took him and the medics into Carden. I guess jumping in with him just sort of washed away some of my frustration; I thought the people there should have done more for him but he seemed quite grateful, though he would have survived had I done nothing. It really was rather stupid of me but it was a beautiful spring day and walking to find the company soon warmed me up.

By the time I got back to the company they had taken the town of Treis and were moving up the hill again to the south. A short time after we topped the hill we hit some light resistance with small arms fire coming from a band of small pines at the edge of an open field. We spread out and opened up with marching fire as we advanced toward the woods. Two tanks behind us were giving supporting fire as we moved but, as we neared the wood, it began coming very close to me and I ran into the woods to get out of the line of fire. The band of pines was dense but not very deep; I could see only a few feet in front of me and suddenly emerged from the pines to find an open wooded area with a shallow ditch just past the pines. I stepped into the ditch unexpectedly and stepped on a German soldier! There were twelve or fifteen German troops lying in the ditch, taking cover from our marching fire. I was just as surprised to find them there as they were to see me. I was on my feet; they were prone facing away from me and I had distinct advantage of position. They were surrendering as the rest of the platoon came up.

At this time I was, so far as I know, the last man in the rifle or weapons platoons who had not been wounded and out of the company for several weeks. Until March 24th there had been four of us, Chaney, Hank, Andy and me. In fact, I think First Sgt. Pierce and I were the only two left in the company who had been in it in Normandy. After eight months we were the survivors, aside from the cooks and company clerk.

Some wonder, when bad things happen to them,"Why me, Lord? Why me?" I wonder "Why me, Lord?" for the opposite reason. Why was I spared?

In the nineteen eighties my wife and I went back to Carden and spent the night. I think my wife remembers that visit from the sleepless night she had as a train seemed to go by the window of our lodging every few minutes during the night. I had the only bad meal I ever had in Germany, sections of very greasy eel.

The vineyard on the south bank is gone, the river has been widened by dam construction , and a large cross has been placed on top of the hill where we fought and where my good friend Hank Terzago died, along with others. I don't know why it was placed there. No one I asked knew but it is a fitting monument to Hank who was a good soldier, always cheerful, a good friend and a fine young man. In my mind the cross is in memory of Hank and the others, American and German, who died there. Whenever I hear O Sole Mio I always think of Hank who sang it often, maybe not as well as Luciano Pavarotti but with as much feeling and enthusiasm. I guess I was, in many ways, closer to him than most of my friends who were killed. I wrote his parents a letter after the war in response to a request in the divisional magazine asking for details about his final days. Thank goodness I didn't have to lie in saying that he was killed instantly. God rest your soul, old friend. After the war I was invited to attend a memorial mass in New Jersey but I didn't go.

I like the quotation in Demille's book *The General's Daughter* regarding Taps.

"It is appropriate that the last call that a soldier hears at night has been chosen to be played over his grave to mark the beginning of the last, long sleep, and to remind those assembled that as the day follows night, so will the final taps be followed by the great reveille to come."

Two thousand years ago Catullus went to the tomb of his brother to pay honor to his memory, stated in this translation of his ode.

> Even so, accept this tradition handed down
> According to old parenteral custom,
> Moist with a brother's tears
> And, forever, brother, hail and farewell.
> The Sharp End, *Ellis,* pp346

Hank and the others were my brothers.

> The muffled drum has beat
> The soldier's last tattoo.
> No more on life's parade shall meet
> The brave and fallen few.
> On fame's eternal camping ground
> Their silent tents are spread

The Second Mosel Crossing

And glory guards, with solemn round
The bivouac of the dead.

Thomas O'Hare The Bivouac of the Dead

The Palatinate Blitz

Shortly thereafter we again mounted on tanks and trucks and swept through the Palatinate area of Germany, moving south and cutting off the Germans remaining in the Siegfried Line. In eight days the regiment took some 52 towns and took about 1000 prisoners, crossing the Hunsruck chain of hills and making crossings of the Nahe and Alsenz rivers en route to the Rhine. The Palatinate campaign was a typical Patton campaign, moving fast, bypassing pockets of resistance and cutting off thousands of Germans, most of whom surrendered. It has been described as a classic military operation. Somewhere along the way, I can't recall the town, we overran a German headquarters and captured several generals who had no idea we were in the area. I took a rather fancy sword from an officer who protested vehemently but futilely. Some of these troops made a point of being Austrian rather than German, as if that made any difference to us. They must have thought we believed Austrians did nothing but dance the "Blue Danube Waltz". Many Austrians were rabid Nazis when all was going well.

The sword wound up, along with some ceremonial daggers and other "souvenirs", in my bedroll and, after I placed it there a few days later, I never saw it again. When a soldier was killed or wounded the people in company headquarters returned personal items to his family and usually distributed souvenirs amongst themselves. It doesn't seem right but it really was about the only option unless the casualty was sent to a nearby hospital and someone from the company could visit him. We were never near a general hospital and had no opportunity to visit hospitalized friends.

On one occasion we spotted a German convoy in a deep valley several hundred yards below and to the south of us as we topped a hill and started to descend into the valley. The armor with us opened up on them at about the time some fighter planes spotted them and began strafing them. They bailed out of their vehicles and we took many prisoners that day. As I recall, they were 17th SS Panzer troops we had several scrapes with before.

Sometime during this campaign Sgt. Steve, an old timer in the company who had been wounded at the base of the thumb in one hand, came back up and received an identical mirror wound at the same place on the other hand.

We had received a new 60 mm. mortar after having one destroyed by enemy fire. It was a new type modeled after the Japanese "knee mortar" and consisted of a tube with no bipod and a very small base plate. The shell was fired by pulling a lanyard which activated a trigger, in contrast to the regular mortar where the shell was detonated by falling on the firing pin. As we walked along a high ridge road one cloudy day we spotted a German soldier walking up a hillside on the opposite ridge. Captain Jones wanted to try the new mortar himself and set it up on the hard shoulder of the road. The recoil kicked it against his thigh with considerable force; he missed the German by a considerable distance. In fact, the soldier just kept walking as if nothing had happened. I suspect he felt that if that's the best they can do I won't worry. The captain was not enthused about the new gun. We weren't either and I think it just disappeared, more or less purposely.

The weather was pleasant, a few spring flowers were in bloom, and our drive through the Hunsruck was a pleasant change from the campaigns in Metz, the Siegfried Line and the Bulge. I suspect there are a number of German civilians who remember us with some degree of hostility. Whenever we could we billeted in homes and it must have been a shock for a German housewife to find her spotless feather beds and comforters soiled beyond belief when we left, after sleeping in our muddy clothes and occasionally with our boots on. We were still fighting a war and had to stand two hours on watch, two off with no chance to undress. We ate a lot of fresh eggs, sometimes a dozen or so at a time. After eating the green, tasteless dehydrated eggs the army provided they were a delight. Occasionally we got some pastry of one sort or another. Delicious! The German people in this largely rural area did not seem to be at all short of food. The eggs were kept in vats of brine and there was plenty of sauerkraut which was easily located by the smell. We cooked domesticated rabbit which were plentiful. There were a number of French prisoners of war who were serving as farm labor in the area. They seemed well fed and fairly content. Some of them also functioned as bedtime companions to the women whose husbands were in service or dead. Not a bad place to spend a war: no fighting, plenty to eat, good German wine and a hausfrau to warm your bed.

On one occasion we had been moving rapidly with little resistance and halted for the day in a small village. Scrounging for food was nonproductive and several of us decided to go to the next village to see if we could find some eggs or pastry. There was an abandoned German motorcycle in the village and I rode it toward the next village. However, as we neared the town I noted that there were no white sheets, signifying surrender, hanging from the windows. In addition no one was visible, usually a sign that there were troops in town preparing to resist. I made a wide turn back to the rear but the motorcycle slipped on the wet steep pavement and fell on top of me. I was unable to turn the motor off and it spun around on top of me. I abandoned it there, as far as I know it is still spinning.

March 17- I'm still in one piece and I ask for nothing more. I'm feeling well, just finished a good meal of fried potatoes, ham and fresh eggs and it's really good after K rations. This war has really knocked a big hole in my life. A lot of things will seem childish and senseless to me but don't worry, I'll make the change (to civilian life) without clashing gears a bit. This war can end any day now, I've got a good watch and a Luger from Jerry.

I'm sending a 1000 mark note in this letter, light a cigar with it, that's all it's good for.

March 22,1945- I hope the weather at home is as nice as it is here. The sun is out, not a cloud in the sky and the trees are beginning to bud out. Wish I could be home sitting on the river bank pretending I'm fishing. I've found a sure cure for fish that won't bite, just takes one hand grenade and it's yours for keeps. I'm trying to send home a dress sword but it's over 36 inches long and they won't let me send it. I'm sending you a German bayonet. I've picked up a 7.65 Hungarian pistol I really like. This "blitz" business is far better than the slug it out infantry fighting. We get much more loot when we hit Jerry when he's not expecting us. I got four pistols, three rifles and a swastika flag in one room the other day, also some flashy Kraut uniforms.

A Company boarding pontoon ferry on the Rhine

A Company jeeps at Nierstein on the east bank of the Rhine

The Rhine Crossing

On the morning of March 22nd we moved by truck to an airstrip in the hilly area on the west bank of the Rhine. The plan was for all of the Third Army's artillery spotter planes, light two seater planes of the Piper Cub type, facetiously called Maytag Messerschmitts, to ferry A Company across the river, landing at an airstrip on the east bank of the Rhine. The code name of the plan was Operation Grasshopper. The planes held only the pilot and one passenger, usually an artillery observer, so the planes would have to make at least 150 to 200 landings under fire and would not stop to let an infantryman out but would slow down to let him jump out while still rolling and quickly take off again. Those of us in the weapons platoon thought this idea was insane. Imagine jumping out of a small door from a rolling airplane with a 60+ pound packboard on your back, so bulky it would be difficult to exit, or carrying a 42 pound mortar with no ammunition to fire after you got out! It was much the same in the machine gun section; the gun was carried by two men and the ammunition by two others. The presence or absence of covering enemy troops at the airfield on the east bank was unknown. Needless to say we were not wildly enthused about that idea and would probably have lynched the originator of the idea had he been around. None the less the small planes began to assemble on the field, our will be damned.

The 5th Division reached the Rhine at Nierstein, between Worms and Mainz, on March 22nd. We had with us a detachment of the Navy with motorized landing craft. The initial crossing was made the evening we reached the river by K Company of the 11th Infantry who paddled across the 800 foot wide river in rubber assault boats without a shot being fired. It was the first time in recorded history that a crossing of the Rhine had been performed in assault boats. They were followed by the motorized naval LCVP (Landing Craft Vehicle Personnel) and pontoon rafts; the beachhead was firmly established by dawn. However the crossing to the south near Oppenheim was made under heavy machine gun fire but with only moderate casualties. The Piper Cub airborne assault was cancelled, thank goodness!

A Company moved down to the river the morning of the 23rd. The west bank is quite hilly, the east bank low and level, so that we had good observation of activity on the far bank. A number of antiaircraft batteries were set up on the high ground, commanding the landing site, but they really were not prepared for what followed that afternoon. We loaded into pontoon rafts and were ferried across the river, then pushed through the 11th Infantry and attacked toward the north. At about four o'clock that afternoon we were pinned down for several minutes by machine gun and small arms fire; as fate would have it, on the airstrip we were supposed to land on in the small planes. It would have been a disaster had the plan been followed. While on the airstrip we took some enemy 80 mm. mortar fire and returned it with 60 mm. mortar fire, with what results I don't know. It may have been effective-after we fired a few rounds they shut up. There was moderate small arms fire as well as the mortar fire.

During the time we were moving through the 11th Infantry we were strafed by Focke Wulfe fighters but the big surprise was the appearance of ME -262s, the German jet which was the first jet ever flown in combat. They came over strafing at an altitude of about 300 feet. They were much faster than anything we had seen before and we, trying to locate them by sound, looked for them far behind their actual position. The plane was far ahead of the sound that we were accustomed to. The antiaircraft fire was far behind them. Luckily for us, the planes tended to direct their fire toward the landing zones where the engineers were constructing a treadway bridge.The anti aircraft fire from the west bank shot down six FW -109s but probably never came near the 262s. It was, as far as I know, the first time the ME -262s had been used against us and they were impressive. If Hitler had pushed their construction we probably would have had to call off the bombing of Germany as our fighters would have been no match for them, being completely outclassed in terms of speed.

Later in the evening we moved into Astheim, a small crossroad town, against sporadic opposition. The mortar section set up the guns in a garden area, enclosed by brick walls, behind a one story building. One of our tanks pulled up at a "Y" road fork in front of the house. As darkness fell we began looking for something to eat and discovered some black bread and delicious strawberry preserves as well as the usual eggs in brine. We left one man out with the guns while the rest of us prepared to feast; an absolutely stupid thing to do but since there were friendly troops on all four sides of us we felt secure. Usually we kept one man on each mortar in a combat situation no matter how quiet it was but this time we ignored the fact that we had to fight to get into the town.

While we were taking care of our appetites and ignoring any threat to life a Panzerfaust, the German equivalent of our antitank bazooka, slammed into the rear of the tank parked not fifteen feet from us and it exploded into flames. The party was over! At the same time several Germans came over the wall into the small area where the mortars were set up. We came out of the kitchen in a hurry and cleared the area of the Krauts but it was touch and go for a while. I think most of them made it back over the wall. The civilians in the house had been in a covered cellar, used to store potatoes, cabbage, apples etc., in the side yard of the house. We would duck in there intermittently when sporadic shelling of the area began.

The Germans had infiltrated the town in two company strength, cutting off the battalion headquarters in the center of town from the rifle companies on the periphery. In fact, the battalion aid station was set up in a house which turned out to have seven German soldiers in it. Luckily, they surrendered at daylight. Needless to say, it was a confused and hectic situation. The mortar section was intermittently out of contact with the rest of the company. German tanks were active in the area but did not venture into town. We in the mortar section had no fire from them while the rifle platoons on the periphery did. The rifle companies had to turn around and attack toward battalion headquarters. The mortar section was given the task of guarding alleyways in the town to prevent enemy movement. The situation throughout the night remained confused for as fast as we cleared a section of town more Germans would infiltrate in from an estimated two companies in the surrounding fields.

Apple Blossom Time

I have a rendezvous with death
At some disputed barricade,
When apple blossoms fill the air
And springtime comes with rustling shade.

Joyce Kilmer

That is a little melodramatic and I obviously didn't die but it was close.

Shortly after daylight Captain Jones assembled a twenty man force to go, with two of our tanks, into the fields around the town and clear the surrounding area of Germans. As we cleared areas in the town during the night other Germans would slip in from the fields and reoccupy cleared areas. Frank Brickman was an old timer in the company who had been wounded in Normandy and was just returning to the company. He and I were detailed to be in the assault group. Captain Jones led the group, characteristic of him. He knew it would be a rough assignment and he did not give it to a platoon leader as he could have.

It was a beautiful clear morning, blue skies and light white clouds, a gorgeous spring day. We formed up on the edge of town and moved to the north through an orchard. I don't know whether the trees were apple or pear but the blossoms were white and in full bloom. The "rendezvous with death" bit obviously came to mind. We all knew the war was coming to an end, which made every attack that much harder, but each attack had to be done to complete our mission. As far as I was concerned the worst part of the whole thing was that I was armed only with a .45 pistol with an effective range of, with luck, 50 feet or so and we were going against machine guns, tanks and rifles. I was a squad leader at the time but that morning we were shorthanded and I had been acting as a gunner and did not have the carbine a squad leader usually carried. My best hope was to pick up a rifle from the first casualty. There was absolutely no cover, freshly plowed level ground with very shallow furrows. At the time I was hit in November I had a definite premonition of disaster and, on this morning, I felt that I would almost certainly be hit. There was too little cover and too many Krauts. Frank and I both felt the same way and talked about it briefly.

We split into two groups: one tank with half the infantry in front firing to the front and into the fields on the left; the other, somewhat to the right near the town, firing into the German occupied sector of the town. We tried to shelter behind the tanks as much as possible but there was enemy fire coming from both flanks and the front.

Frank and I got behind the second tank as we moved out. We would step out from behind the tank and fire to the front or side as targets presented themselves to us, usually just firing toward likely areas where the enemy may be. The tanks were firing machine guns as we moved. We had gone several hundred yards when I saw a German crawling in a ditch about 100 yards away, too far for me to hit with the pistol. I pointed him out to one of the riflemen who fired several times at him. It has haunted me to some degree as I have thought, in retrospect, that he may have been wounded and we usually tended to spare Germans we knew were wounded.

It may come as a surprise to some, in view of German atrocities known at the time, but most of us felt a good deal of respect and sympathy for the average German soldier. Many of them were there whether they wanted to be or not and suffered the same hardships we did. Some of them were quite arrogant and obnoxious, even as prisoners, and some of them may not have made it back to the prisoner cages alive. We occasionally, rarely I should say, got the order to take no prisoners if we had to move fast and did not have enough men to escort prisoners to the rear. In those circumstances we would sometimes disarm them and wave them to the rear, unescorted. That usually worked quite well toward the end of the war. Most of them knew the war was lost and were glad to be out of it. That "no prisoners" order was routinely ignored as they would fight to the death if they saw someone shot who was trying to surrender. If the order was followed we would lose more men. One of the few exceptions when surrendering Germans were sometimes shot occurred when a well defended machine gun position would fire until their ammunition was expended, killing lots of us, and then surrender.

Shortly thereafter we began receiving artillery fire to our front, whether ours or Jerry's I don't know but it was close enough to place shrapnel around us. Frank stepped to the right to fire into the town and was immediately hit in the abdomen. I stopped to see about his injury, ascertained that he had a serious wound, and moved him into the deepest furrow I could find as the shelling and small arms fire incoming was troublesome.

I ran three or four steps to get back behind the tank when I saw dirt kicking up from machine gun fire from my right front striking the ground and coming directly at me. A blow in my left leg knocked me off of my feet and I fell prone onto the ground. I immediately tried to get up and run but my leg would not hold me up and I fell again. It was my turn!

Surprisingly, there was relatively little pain at the time. Maybe I was so preoccupied with staying alive that I didn't notice the pain much. Jerry fired another burst of machine gun fire at me and shot the heel off the boot on my right foot. I couldn't figure out why they were such bad shots as the fire was coming from a house cellar not over 50 yards from me. I could clearly see the men shooting at me. At any rate, I decided the best thing to do was play dead. The tanks and the rest of the men moved on around the edge of the town. Things then quieted down in my area though I could hear the progress of the force as they circled the town and there was sporadic fire in the town as buildings were being cleared.

After a few minutes a German soldier came out of the building that housed the men who had shot me. He started out in the field toward Frank and me, carrying a Schmeisser machine pistol. My face was turned in his direction and I could see him quite clearly. I didn't know whether to try to shoot him with my pistol or just play dead but I knew I had little chance of hitting him. He was close enough to hit me with ease so I continued to play dead. As he walked toward us one of our riflemen on the perimeter of town several hundred yards away fired a single shot , hitting the German in the head and killing him instantly.

Shortly thereafter one of our medics, a boy named Baker from Hazard, Kentucky, came walking out to check Frank and me. He had his Red Cross helmet marker and arm band on. The Germans usually respected it, as they did on this occasion, and he came by and spoke to Frank, telling him not to move. He came up to me as I continued to play dead but spoke to him. He lifted my head and let it drop, as if I were dead, to continue the charade. Then he walked over to the building where the Germans were who had shot me and talked them into surrendering as it was, by now, obvious that the town was being cleared of Germans. They consented to do so and five or six of them came out and the same ones that shot me carried me into the house they had been in. The medic dressed my leg and gave me a shot of morphine. They also brought Frank Brickman into the building. I gave some civilians in the house some powdered coffee and they gave me some pastry. We carried on a rather idiotic conversation in broken German and English about the stupidity of war. About all the German I knew was "Krieg nicht gut" (War is bad) and their English was not much better.

After an hour or so some of our medics came by and took me in a jeep to the aid station. There they put a splint on my leg, gave me another shot and loaded me into an ambulance. We made our way back to the beachhead landing site and waited for a LCVP to carry the ambulance back across the river. There were several walking wounded sitting on a bench along the right side of the ambulance, I was on the bottom stretcher on the left, a wounded German was in the stretcher above me. It took a long time to get back to the 104th Evacuation Hospital in Trier. The morphine wore off and my leg, for the first time, became very painful. The splint was very tight and uncomfortable. The Kraut in the stretcher over me began to say "To piss, to piss" and I couldn't get the drivers to stop. Finally the German could it hold it no longer and I became a great deal wetter than I had been when the trip began. An ignominious way to end a war! The winners should piss on the losers, not the other way round.

We came into Trier sometime after dark. As I was admitted to the hospital they brought in Captain Jones, who had also been wounded. He told me that all of the infantry in our miniassault force had been wounded but no one had been killed. The attack was a success as the fields and town had been cleared of the enemy.

At the hospital they loosened my splint which helped a great deal but one of the major arteries supplying my leg had been interrupted and a surgeon told me that he may have to amputate my leg just above the ankle. However, after a spinal anesthetic the blood supply improved, the wound was cleaned up and the leg placed in a cast. After a day or so in a hospital tent I was loaded into a C-47 (DC3) transport and flown to Bournemouth on the south coast of England to enter the 104th General Hospital.

I spent my twentieth birthday in a ward in England with thirty or forty other wounded men. While there I had a skin graft taken from my right thigh to cover the wound in my left leg, but it failed to take and it was five months before the area on my leg granulated in and closed. Oddly enough, the graft area hurt more than the gunshot. The deep peroneal nerve had been severed and I was unable dorsiflex my foot (move my foot toward the front of my leg), a condition called a drop foot.

The stay in the hospital was relatively pleasant except for the fact that I had a shot of penicillin every three hours. It was still crude stuff at the time. I understood that in some hospitals they were collecting patient's urine and extracting penicillin for reuse but not in the 104th Hospital. I did feel like a human pin cushion.

Bed baths by a very attractive black headed nurse often resulted in visible evidence of masculine eroticism. This was quickly terminated without any comment on her part by a sharp flick of a fingernail directed to the appropriate area. The recipient of this attention occasionally responded with an "Ouch" with laughter from the nearby beds. All hands could empathize.

There were lots of "war stories" swapped while on that ward. Tall tales, reading and listening to the Glenn Miller Band on the Armed Forces Radio made up the sum total of our recreational activity. Irvin Roblewski, the man next to me, was a short, stocky fellow from Milwaukee who had been in an I & R (Intelligence and Reconnaisance) platoon in the 4th Infantry Division. He told a story about a bayonet assault his unit made in Normandy. Before the assault his unit was told that Germans were afraid of cold steel and would flee when they saw the bayonets. As he moved across a field toward the German lines the Germans came out to meet them with fixed bayonets. Irv, who was about five and a half feet tall and weighed no more than 140 pounds , said the Germans all looked like they were seven feet tall. He turned and sought the shelter of the hedgerow he had just left! He was later wounded in Germany and hidden in the attic of a building occupied by German troops for several days before the village fell to the Americans; sheltered by German civilians!

Letter from home, March 24th, 1945-
I guess you are across the Rhine by this time, You must take good care of yourself. It may not be long until the war will end over there. Patton's Army is sure going places. Are you well? The going from now on won't be so bad because the winter is about over and you won't have the ice and cold to worry about. Your last letter was the 13th of February. That's a long time. I'm sure you haven't time to write so often. Be careful son and write when you have a chance.
All my love and good luck,
    Mom.
    April 2- This is the old human sieve writing from merry old England. I was machine gunned in the left leg, broke it near the ankle so I guess I'll be out of action for a while. I hope this is the last Oak Leaf Cluster for my Purple Heart.
    April 18- I'm getting along fine, just lying here listening to Kay Kyser (an American dance band). *This life is a little monotonous but it's safe at least. We even had Coca Cola yesterday. I'll be glad when I can get up in a wheel chair.*
    Thanks for sending the package to me. I doubt if I'll get it as we have an agreement that if one of us gets hit the mail orderly will give it to the rest of the men in the platoon. The best fighting men in the world and I'd rather they'd have it than me. I've got the world on a string even if I did have to get hit to get a break.
    April 10th-I'm getting along OK. I guess it's better being here than up on the line. I'm fairly sure of winning the Battle of the Bedpans. Cheer up the folks at home as much as possible about this thing. It's not a bad wound at all, the fellows back at the company say I've got a "Million Dollar Wound."
    April 28th-Patton's secret weapon was mechanized today, I got up in a wheel chair for the first time and it's really all right. Been all over the ward and had a good time.
    May 5th- Got a stack of letters about two feet high the other day, several from you all. I'm getting along fine, I get around on crutches a little now, Saw my leg yesterday for the first time and one of the wounds has healed up completely. So I guess I'll be up and around in a month or so.
    P.S. Got some good news, never mind writing me for a while.

Home, Sweet Home

Not but wut abstract war is horrid
I sign to that with all my heart.
But civilization doos go forrid
Sometimes upon a powder cart.

J. R. Lowell, Bigelow papers, seri, p.28

The European War ended on May 8th. On that day I was taken down to the waterfront and carried on board the USS T.H.Bliss for transport home. The British people were in the streets en masse, bells ringing, people cheering, lots of drinking etc., horns blowing and who could blame them! One of the British newspapers had a headline "How we, a nation of 40 million, have defeated the mighty Hun." They had a little help but I can understand the feeling.

I was carried on board and down to the ship's hospital in a wire basket which was quite uncomfortable as we went down steep ship's ladders to the ward but I was tickled pink to be there.

Most of the troops on the ship were Americans who had just been released from prisoner of war camps in Germany. They were, by and large, a lean, gaunt looking group. The voyage home took about eleven or twelve days. We were still in convoy in case some diehard Nazis in a submarine might want to make a last effort. I was in the sick bay in the hold of the ship most of the time but one day I was carried up on deck to soak up the warmth of the sun. It was wonderful after the miserable European winter weather.

We docked in Boston and I was taken to Fort Miles Standish for a few days. The high points were the availability of an unlimited supply of milk and a phone call to home! From there I went by train to McClosky General Hospital in Temple, Texas, an amputation and neurosurgical center. The trip was in hospital cars which were set up with beds by large windows, a veritable goldfish bowl with very little privacy. I felt that the cars were designed that way to have some propaganda value-"Look at the poor soldiers etc." to boost the idea that "There's a war going on." Frankly, I resented it at the time, and still do, but at least the view out was unrestricted.

The first day I was permitted to get up on crutches and go to the mess hall on my own I found Orvel Chaney standing in the chow line. Small world.

After a few days in the hospital in Temple I was fitted with a drop foot brace and crutches and furloughed home. I got on a train in Temple and stood

169

up from there to St.Louis, listening to seated civilians complain about the probability that their defence jobs were going to be phased out. I did not have great sympathy for them. In St. Louis I struggled along on crutches for several hundred yards carrying a bulky duffel bag with no offer of help from the civilians in the train depot and, by then, I had practically *no* use for civilians! On the TV program *The World at War* a wounded soldier commented that his surgeon told him the only place you'll find sympathy is in the dictionary, between shit and syphilis. But everyone has their own set of problems.

I caught a bus from St. Louis to Lexington and was met there by my brother Blaine, Dad and Lynn, my nephew who drove me home. When we mounted a hill and rounded a curve we passed a roadside sign that said "Entering Morgan County." For the first time I felt that I was really home. It was over.

After the furlough I was transferred to Nichols General Hospital in Louisville, Kentucky. The atom bombs were dropped, frankly to my great satisfaction as it probably would have cost thousands of American lives to invade Japan. I suspect that very few of those who now condemn the dropping of the bomb were slated to be in the first wave of the invasion forces attacking the Japanese homeland. The war ended while I was in the hospital but the patients were restricted to the base on VJ Day (the day the war ended) and I missed the mass orgy of that day. I was discharged on August 28th and was able to spend six months with my father before he died. My brother Harold came home a few hours after Dad died. Of some interest is the fact that Harold did the discharge physical examaination on Admiral Doenitz, the Nazi who became Hitler's successor, for the German Navy.

I went back to school, getting a B.S. degree from the University of Kentucky and an M.D. from the University of Louisville. Andy Carpenter was a patient of mine when I did general practice in Owingsville, Kentucky. I understand Andy died recently. Orvel Chaney still lives and farms on Grassy Creek in Morgan County. He married a woman whose husband was killed while serving in the 95th Division near Metz. I just recently discovered that she and I are somewhat distantly related cousins.

After a few years in general practice I specialized in radiology and have practiced in Maury County, Tennessee for the past thirty years. My leg wound healed fairly completely but I have never been able to run very well since it happened, small price to pay for survival.

I have been incredibly lucky.

The drums are silent now.

Epilogue

When after many battles past, Both, tir'd with blows, make peace
    at last,
What is it, after all, the people get?
Why! Taxes, widows, wooden legs and debt.
    Francis Moore, Almanac, Observations for 1829, pp.23

Once you have lain in the arms of war you can admit no other mistress.
You may loathe her but you cannot deny her. No lover can offer you
defter caresses, more exquisite torture, such peaking delight. No wine
gives fiercer intoxication, no drug more vivid exhaltation. Those who
hate her most are prisoners to her spell. They rise from her embrace
pillaged, soiled, maybe ashamed but they are hers.
    Siegfried Sasson-"A Passionate Prodigy"

Do you believe that?

When all else has been forgotten the abiding lesson of combat in World
War Two is the fact that in the midst of seeming chaos it was the love
of individuals, one for another, that enabled them to carry on. The
fighting soldiers were sustained by a regard for others in which self
respect and mutual esteem were so inextricably intertwined that courage was a commonplace, self sacrifice the norm. Without this bedrock
of genuine human love there would have been no combat divisions,
not a billion cheery exhortations, a million sergeant-majors or a thousand scaffolds could have made a jot of difference. At the last extreme
of the human spirit men turn to those nearest them for reassurance as
to their own plight and of the continued existence of common human-
ity. At the sharp end few men turned in vain.
    The Sharp End-*John Ellis*-1980

Ellis also comments that "It is not only observers who commented on the
vital importance of emotional ties among the men. Almost all participants'
accounts mention it and often regret that this sense of comradeship had no real
equivalence in peacetime."

And who is right? Moore, Sasson or Ellis? Or all three?

"There's one thing you can say when it's all over and you're home once more. You can thank God when you're sitting by the fireside with your grandson on your knee, and he asks you what you did in the war, you won't have to shift him to your other knee , cough and say "I shoveled shit in Louisiana."

General Patton ,1944

God and the soldier do all men adore
In time of trouble but no more.
For when the war is over
And all the wrongs are righted
God is forgotten and the soldier slighted.

U S Army training manual

In 1993, how true.

B. H. Liddell Hart, the acknowledged leading military historian of the Second World War era, has the following to say on the opening page of his *History of the Second World War-*

"The Western Allies entered that war with a two-fold object. The immediate objective was to fulfill their promise to preserve the independence of Poland. The ultimate purpose was to remove a potential menace to themselves, and thus secure their own security. In the outcome, they failed in both purposes."

After the apparent victory we acquiesced in Russia's domination of Poland and faced a fresh and greater menace, the Soviet Union. This and past experience dispelled the popular illusion that "victory" spells peace. It has taken another fifty years for the "Cold War" to wind down and, with the current instability in Russia, that may be an illusion.

Only the dead have seen the last of war.

Plato

HEADQUARTERS FIFTEENTH U. S. ARMY
Office of the Commanding General
A P O 408

17 November, 1945

To the Officers and Men of the Fifth Infantry Division:

Nothing I can say can add to the glory which you have achieved.

Throughout the whole advance across France you spearheaded the attack of your Corps. You crossed so many rivers that I am persuaded many of you have web feet and I know that all of you have dauntless spirit. To my mind history does not record incidents of greater valor than your assault crossings of the Sauer and the Rhine.

Concerning the former operation, I showed the scene of your glorious exploit to a civilian for whom I have the highest esteem. After looking at it for some time he said, "I did not believe there was enough courage in the world to achieve such a victory." Knowing the Fifth Infantry Division, I was sure you would achieve it and you did.

Now that peace has been re-established I am sure all of you will continue through the remainder of your lives to stand for those great qualities of America which in war you so magnificently demonstrated.

With affectionate regards and sincere congratulations, I am, as ever,

Your devoted commander,

G. S. Patton

G. S. PATTON, JR.
General